One of the most celebrated names of football writing, Arthur Hopcraft was witness to many of the highlights of the English game, which he wrote about with unreserved passion and intelligence. A successful and highly revered writer and journalist, he was also the *Guardian*'s feature writer and a prolific scriptwriter. Among his best-known works is his adaptation of John le Carré's *Tinker, Tailor, Soldier, Spy* (1979). He also wrote the screenplays for *Agatha* (1979), *Hard Times* (1977), *A Tale of Two Cities* (1989) and *Rebecca* (1996), and won the Bafta's Writer's Award in 1985. Born on 20 November 1932 in Shoeburyness, Essex, he grew up in Cannock, Staffordshire. He died on 22 November 2004.

The Football Man

People and Passions in Soccer

Arthur Hopcraft

With a new foreword by Michael Parkinson

Contents

Author's Acknowledgements

Some sections of this book have been developed from articles which I originally wrote for the sports pages of the *Observer* and for the *Sunday Times Magazine*, and I am grateful to the editors of both for allowing me to call on this material.

Foreword

I first met Arthur Hopcraft when we worked together on a local paper in Barnsley. He was the first reporter I had encountered who wore a bow tie, which took courage in Barnsley in the 1950s. We shared a love of football and both wrote the occasional report on Barnsley F.C. We fancied ourselves as football writers rather than football reporters and showed off shamelessly.

My most ambitious attempt to enter the 'Dictionary of Deathless Prose' occurred when I noticed that one of the Barnsley players bore a distinct resemblance to Scott Fitzgerald, whose photograph I had seen in a paperback version of *The Great Gatsby*. I wrote something like 'Roy Cooling was Barnsley's best player. Cooling, who bears a remarkable resemblance to Scott Fitzgerald…' This came out in the paper as 'Cooling, who bears a remarkable resemblance to Scott of the Antarctic'. When I asked what had happened the editor said they had changed the name because no one in Barnsley had heard of Scott Fitzgerald, whereas everyone knew the explorer.

I moved on and so did Arthur. We next worked together at Granada TV in Manchester. It was the time of Busby and Best and Arthur started writing the odd piece for the *Observer*. He did his best work at this time. His profile of George Best, reprinted in the book, is wonderful journalism, carefully crafted and impeccably researched. It is his signature piece, yet the book is full of writing of similar quality. It was a time of change in society as well as football and Hopcraft, with his ability to see the game against the agitated background of the community it served, was a perceptive and gifted observer.

He later gained acclaim for the plays and adaptations he wrote for television, among them John le Carré's *Tinker, Tailor, Soldier, Spy*. At his memorial service le Carré spoke warmly of Arthur's meticulous and sensitive adaptation of his novel.

Because football was always his hobby and never his business Arthur retained his ability to see the game clearly, blemishes and all. He was a reporter with a shrewd eye as well as being a writer of elegance. He was my friend and I am delighted he is being both remembered and celebrated by the republication of *The Football Man*. It in no way embraces all his talents as a writer yet is clearly an outstanding example of his gifts as a journalist.

Some say it is the best book written about the game. It is certainly as good as the best and I can't think of a better one.

Michael Parkinson
November 2005

Introduction

The point about football in Britain is that it is not just a sport people take to, like cricket or tennis or running long distances. It is inherent in the people. It is built into the urban psyche, as much a common experience to our children as are uncles and school. It is not a phenomenon; it is an everyday matter. There is more eccentricity in deliberately disregarding it than in devoting a life to it. It has more significance in the national character than theatre has. Its sudden withdrawal from the people would bring deeper disconsolation than to deprive them of television. The way we play the game, organize it and reward it reflects the kind of community we are.

No player, manager, director or fan who understands football, either through his intellect or his nerve-ends, ever repeats that piece of nonsense trotted out mindlessly by the fearful every now and again which pleads, 'After all, it's only a game.' It has not been only a game for eighty years: not since the working classes saw in it an escape route out of drudgery and claimed it as their own. It has not been a sideshow this century. What happens on the football field matters, not in the way that food matters but as poetry does to some people and alcohol does to others: it engages the personality. It has conflict and beauty, and when those two qualities are present together in something offered for public appraisal they represent much of what I understand to be art. The people own this art in the way they can never own any form of music, theatre, literature or religion because they cannot be fooled in it as they can in these other things, where intention can be deliberately obscured and method hidden beyond their grasp. Football does not ask for faith; it compels examination. Phoney footballers are simply booted aside. The crowds can be vindictive and brutal, but they can seldom be deceived. They know about their football intuitively, as they know about their families.

My aim in this book is to explore the character of football: to consider its effects on people's lives. I hope that I can explain something of football's compulsion.

The book will, of course, be heavily informed by personal preferences, particularly when I am writing about players and methods of play. There is no such animal as a totally objective football fan. If a man's natural inclination is towards the imaginative rather than the combative he is never going to accept that Nobby Stiles could be a better halfback than Danny Blanchflower. But in the main in this book I am more concerned with people than with technique.

Some readers are going to be offended by the omission of some of their favourite names in football. But this is not a gallery of heroes. I am a reporter trying to reach to the heart of what football is.

1 The Player

1 Georgie

Sport can be cruel to men. Football can make a man more ridiculous even than drink can. Outside the players' entrance at Old Trafford, Manchester United's ground, on a raw and turbulent March morning, the wind blew an old man teetering across the tarmac, wet and flapping in his overcoat like an escaped poster, and draped him across the windows of my car. His fingers rattled on the glass and he was shouting urgently. He was a thin old man with stubble on his chin and a neck like a cockerel's. There were three people in the car, but he was concerned with only one, the boy in the back who was slight and aged 18 and who looked no older. The old man shoved his head into the car as I wound the window down and he gabbled through a breathless rigmarole directed solely at the youth. It was one of those football followers' riddles which hinge on one of the laws of the game, in which some improbable incident is invented, such as the collapsing of the ball as it enters the goal, and the questioner challenges for the correct referee's ruling. This particular problem was incomprehensible in the old man's hoarseness and anxiety. He kept breaking off to shout: 'I was a referee, you know.' The last time he said it he stopped talking altogether, and the boy he was trying to impress, George Best, of United and Northern Ireland, smiled gently at him and said, 'Cheerio,' and we drove away. Best said: 'It happens all the time now.' Then he put a sweet into his mouth, and his face assumed that seamless, private thoughtfulness with which the decently mannered young excuse themselves from contact with an older generation.

This was the diffident, delicate-looking Best of 1965, not at all self-confident in strangers' company. He spoke when he was spoken to, not at all fluently; the voice came haltingly and sounded barely broken. He bit his lower lip a lot, and looked shyly at his interviewer's breast pocket or over his forehead. He was so unused to being interviewed, or to talking to people outside his immediate circle of friends and fellow players, that we had a substantial problem in communication: not just in terms of words but in the fundamental matter of intention. After about an hour of trying to coax some personal information out of him, and getting little but nods and smiles, I said: 'Well, you're not going to get big-headed, are you?' It was expressed as a rueful kind of compliment. There was an instant blush from him and a flash of temper in his eyes, the first spurt of the pulse I had seen from him off the football field. He had clearly taken the observation as an unwelcome injunction from someone not qualified to give it.

Best at this stage, after one season in First Division football, was already being called 'a great player' by United's manager, Matt Busby, and he was already the particular darling of the teenagers among United's supporters. As a piece of football property he must have been worth £100,000 – his market value must be twice that now – and he was earning over £100 a week in the weeks when he played more than once. His own generation was adoring him, girls shrieking his name in the street and writing him letters by the score. Some offered him their company for an evening. One little group delivered to the club a home-iced fruit cake with his name embossed on it, and there was a steady trickle of schoolgirls knocking on the door at his digs, looking for his smile and his autograph.

But so far he was still publicly unobtrusive. He had a small car, which he could not drive, and his face was much more familiar to the readers of the teenagers' pop music magazines than to Manchester's night life. He was immediately recognizable as one of the adolescence movement's first representatives, wearing conspicuous tight suits and pointed shoes and lavishing attention on his abundant hair. He thought the Rolling Stones' music was a much more exciting sound than the Beatles', and he appeared to have an inexhaustible appetite for sweets, ginger cake and horror comics. On the side table under the front-room window of the council house where he lived there was a scrap-book with 'George Best' written in a careful, round hand, and in it were a lot of newspaper pictures of him in action with his socks rolled down.

Mrs Mary Fullaway, his landlady, talked to me about him with much affection. She had looked after him since he first arrived in Manchester from Belfast when he was 15. He was then 5 foot 3 inches tall and weighed four pounds under eight stone, fully dressed. He was with another Irish boy of the same age who had been recommended to Busby, and they were delivered to Mrs Fullaway by car. She remembered seeing 'two little heads through the car window, and saying to myself: "Well, they'll never make footballers".' She put them in twin beds, and the next morning Best's friend said he wanted to go home. Best said: 'We'd agreed that if one of us didn't like it we'd both go back. So we went back on the night boat.'

Two weeks later, after an exchange of letters between Busby and Best's father, George was home again with Mrs Fullaway. 'Puny' was Busby's word for him then. He was found a job as an office boy near to the ground until he signed for the club as

a professional at 17. Four months after his 17th birthday he
played his first League game for United, at outside-right against
West Bromwich Albion. This was one of the two most memorable first appearances I have seen in League football, the other
being that made by Francis Lee on the right wing for Bolton,
who, when he was 15, scored a goal, had his name taken by the
referee and was comforted in his tears by the former England
centre-forward, Nat Lofthouse. (Football fiction is seldom more
extraordinary than its fact.) There was nothing for Best to sniff
about, even though he was so firmly handled by Albion's Welsh
international left-back, Gerry Williams, that Busby moved him
to the other wing for the second half.

Talking about that first game from his position as an 18-year-
old international player, Best said he wished Busby had let him
face Williams all through the match. 'I'd got a knock on the
ankle,' he said, with every indication that he still smarted at the
episode and felt he needed to justify himself. The memory Best
left in my mind after the game was of frailty animated into
intensely personal enterprise. Then, as now, his first concern
was to play the ball at close quarters past whatever grouping of
the opposition stood in his way. This might have been common
enough fifteen or twenty years before, when Stanley Matthews
and Len Shackleton were dancing past static, heavyweight
backs, but in the mid-1960s when the all-purpose, ever-moving
player had rendered such specialization obsolete Best was as
much a surprise as if he had been striking the ball with a hockey-
stick. Best's arrival in League football brought back the verb 'to
dribble' to the sportswriter's vocabulary.

Very quickly after his first game he was established as one of
the leading attractions in football. He showed the startlingly
inventive quality which only the great players have, and one
of the images he created for football followers to carry for ever

in their minds was of this muddy, childlike figure, his hair like a wet, black conifer, holding one of his boots in the air at shoulder height and hitting the ball with his stockinged foot to make a pass that brought United a goal. Some of his mail the next week was addressed to The Bootless Wonder; football fans never miss a cue.

At this time he was living the traditional British footballer's life of training in the morning and loafing the rest of the day. Two nights a week he was satisfying the requirement of his station as a 'living teenage legend' (it is an authentic description, which I have borrowed from an articulate pop singer) by appearing at one or other of Manchester's non-alcoholic beat music clubs. On Monday afternoons he was usually in a snooker hall, nodding at, and seldom replying to, the advice and the bantering insult which came from the crowd of regulars gathered around the table to watch him play inexpertly but solemnly. He was spending about £10 a week, sending money home to his parents and thinking of opening a sports goods shop after he had reached the distant decrepitude of 21.

A little less than three years later, that important birthday passed, Best was still living in Mrs Fullaway's house in the little cul-de-sac with the privet hedges and the daffodils, along with David Sadler, a team-mate and England's new centre-half, but most other aspects of his life off the football field had changed utterly. The feckless, shy charm had been replaced by a more assured kind; there was usually some lovely, thoroughly up-to-date girl at his side when he was seen out after dark; he was driving a white Jaguar; he was the principal of George Best Enterprises and George Best Associates; he was thinking of opening a kind of personal secretariat in Manchester, an office whose staff would apply themselves solely to looking after his fan mail and his diary and all those troublesome, tiresome little matters, such as insurance and driving licences, which are so tedious to busy luminaries.

George, the precocious kid, had become Georgie, the public figure. If you say the word 'Georgie' in Manchester, at any time and in any place, or in close proximity to some kind of football activity in any other British town, nobody is going to ask for the second name. (This applies also to 'Matt', for Busby, 'Denis', for Law, and 'Nobby', for Stiles, and is explained not by the fanaticism of football following but by the deep and lasting impact made by men of extraordinary personality in the context of the sport.) Best by now had been asked on television whether he regarded himself as conceited, and had been told by a newspaper, confiding the information to several million readers, that it appeared that he was. He had been repetitively described in print as 'a genius', and had been courted persistently by a recording company which wanted him to make a pop record for a fee of £7,000. He was tempted, but Busby persuaded him out of it. 'The boss said, "Don't you think you've got enough with the shop and the football?",' Best recalled, and if he remembered the words accurately I did not feel that his delivery quite caught the inexorable edge of his manager's tone for such incidents.

His mail now was seldom less than 150 letters for the first two days of every week, and after one international match it reached 300 letters a day for half a week. A good 70 per cent came from girls, and while most letters were short requests for photographs and for information about his physical characteristics, some might be twelve pages long and packed with detail about mum's new hair-do, the death of the neighbour's dog and the nastiness of the machine-shop foreman. There were more callers than ever, a mixture of mini-skirts and school satchels, at Mrs Fullaway's front door. The burden of an increasing proportion of the attention from girls was: 'Georgie, will you take me out?' If Best was a young man of deep Baptist church commitment, or had a cleft palate to inhibit him, or was abnormally cold to girls through inner confusion, such adoration would not affect him much. But none of these crosses is on his shoulders. He is a girls' pin-up, he is one of the smartest movers outside the cat world and he finds female company a welcome change from being kicked on the shins and elbowed in the throat in pouring rain. He said to me: 'Sometimes I think it would be nice to get married and settle down, but,' and here his eyes wandered away to flicker fondness along the length of the Jaguar, 'there's a long time for that, isn't there?'

His play by late 1967 had developed into the most exciting individual contribution to football on view in Europe, with the arguable exception of that of Portugal's Eusebio. (In May 1968, he was voted British Footballer of the Year – the youngest ever.) He had added hardly any weight in three years but a little height and much toughness. There was an undoubted flare of ill-temper when tackling and obstruction, often brutal, frustrated him, and he was being berated in the papers and on the terraces for it. But no other virtuoso could now match his range, and it was this variety of talents which had made him so important: the demonic, barely credible capacity for forcing his way out of a ring of defenders, when he might lose the ball and regain it so that the tackle became part of his dribble; his courage in a crowded goalmouth, allowing him to head goals against much bigger men; his inspired eye for a long ball from a deep position behind him. With all this there was a relish for action. Some people were now calling him a playboy; but no playboy was ever more captive to his craft.

The sports shop which the adolescent Best had in mind had not materialized. Instead there were now two shops selling young men's clothes neither sedate nor cheap, one of them called 'Edwardia' and styled astutely in the manner of Best's personal, conscious flair for appearances, with massive football pictures on the walls and silk in the window. There was also a part of a shoeshop whose other principal was Best's friend Mike Summerbee, the Manchester City centre-forward. Best said his main contribution to the running of these shops was to help select the goods.

I saw him in one of his shops wearing a cowboy hat, which he took off quickly in embarrassment. Briefly he had worn a dangling Mexican moustache, which he shaved off because it was uncomfortable when wet, and a chinstrap beard. Every new adornment was photographed by the papers, adding to the growing imagery of a self-regarding, privileged, arrogant young meteor, vibrant on the crest of his trajectory and threatened by an early exhaustion of flame. An early morning collision in the white care not two days before a Saturday match prompted more questions about how seriously he was taking his trade.

But Best is not fundamentally ostentatious; he is merely young, popular, and rich by lower-middle-class standards. It is only because the pay and working conditions of leading profes-sional footballers were so recently those of moderately skilled factory helots that Best and his contemporaries look so exces-sively and immodestly affluent. Seeing him pressing bottles of wine into people's hands at an impromptu party after a match, then stepping jauntily out with a delicious girl in fluffy furs, I was struck by his bravura and his enjoyment of the spotlight. He was not hogging it, but acknowledging its presence while it burned for him. He plays the kind of football he plays because of the kind of person he is.

In one of Mrs Fullaway's armchairs and with her spaniel on

his feet just before teatime he looked glad for the respite from the action. He appeared to know himself shrewdly. He had never moved from his digs because 'it's something normal to come back to if you've been off the rails a bit'.

He talked a little more easily than he had three years before, but still not comfortably, the ambiguous phrases broken up with shrugs and smiles. The tension among the players before matches was increasing all the time, he said. He had his own way of dealing with it. While most of the team were fretting in the dressing-room, taking off a shoe, then walking around, undoing a button, taking another walk, he would stand outside the players' entrance talking to friends. Not until a few minutes before the kick-off would he hurry into the dressing-room and change quickly. 'The boss usually comes to call me,' he said, casually making a remarkable comment on the patience and realistic approach of one of the most acclaimed men in football.

The snooker games had been expunged from the weekly routine; he admitted to drinking wine, and said that avoiding the volume of booze offered to him by people encountered in licensed premises presented a problem in diplomacy; at least he indicated it, and nodded when I put the matter that way. He never went out with a girl on Saturday nights, after matches. For one thing Saturday night was unimaginable as anything other than a night out with the boys; secondly, he could be tired and in a bad temper if the game had been a rough one. He and Summerbee often spent Friday nights watching Third Division football, starring Stockport County. 'I usually start by watching one particular player and end up watching the referee.'

On the town the Best entourage is glamorous and noisy. Jewellery glitters, silk collides with fur, faces are instantly recognized as belonging to the famous; anyone over 30 is treated with crushing consideration. When the conversation lurches away from football it begins to whirl in the mystifying realms of pop music, whose language shuts out strangers as completely as silence. For one moment I thought I saw Georgie collecting somebody's autograph; actually he was taking a pop singer's address.

2 Lineage

How far do we have to go back before we find the direct progenitor of the kind of footballer exemplified by Best? It is a complex matter because we are not dealing solely with style of play but also with the style and substance of the man, as affected by the game. I think the two points most central to the question are how much the game informs his everyday life and how much it pays him. What we are looking for is the first man who owed his identity to football and could afford to flaunt it.

We do not find such a man when we look at the dignified faces surrounding the birth of organized football in 1863, when the old boys' clubs of the public schools needed to standardize the rules. But once an organization existed, with something to be won, if initially only the non-negotiable prestige of championship, the arrival of the professional was assured. Human ambitiousness being what it is, there were bound to be people who would pay money to win acclaim. By the 1880s some of the northern clubs, notably Darwen, Blackburn and Sheffield, were paying their players wages, and once that was made legal the age of the well-bred amateur as a leading footballer was under sentence of death. Playing football was a better way of making a living than sweating in somebody's coalmine or dark, satanic mill. In essence the same argument explains why clever-headed lads turn professional players nowadays rather than go to university and take degrees.

There were no hungry players among those Old Etonians and Old Harrovians and Old Carthusians, but they are worth at least respectful acknowledgement in this context; they did, after all, kick the whole business off. If we examine that handsome scrap-book of Victorian football, entitled *Association Football And The Men Who Made It* (The Caxton Publishing Company), so lovingly mounted by Mr Alfred Gibson and Mr William Pickford, we find that the most celebrated of these amateurs was the centre-forward G. O. Smith. There is a portrait of a pale, thin man seated on a wall, and we are told:

'G.O. had not the physique to play a hard, dashing game had he desired to do so. His gentler methods bore better fruit. He opposed subtlety to force, intellect to mere strength. Slightly over middle height, with a winsome face that bore traces of the pale cast of thought, Smith fought his way to the front by sheer diplomacy. If he could not win by fair means he would not win by foul. Nor did he mind a "charge", provided it was fairly delivered. He did not belong to the drawing-room order of player.'

The public school flavour is rich and nutty here. This is the archetypal Victorian school hero: no coarse bully boy he, nothing crudely or meanly done, he was yet no coward to mind the honest buffets of the world . . . Quite so, Tom Brown.

Smith became headmaster, jointly with another English international player, W. J. Oakley, of a boys' preparatory school, which is something that is certainly not going to happen to, say, Bobby Charlton and Geoff Hurst.

Among the professionals of the period winsomeness of expression gave way to a more menacing look. Here are Mr Gibson and Mr Pickford on Derby County's Stephen Bloomer:

'When his eyes are half-closed then is he most widely awake ... That dash for the goal-line is a Bloomer dash; that single-handed dribble a Bloomer dribble; that fierce rattling shot a Bloomer shot; that superb forward pass is a Bloomer pass; that glorious bid for victory in the eleventh hour is the consummation of Bloomer's art. He has made himself the power he is and has been by reason of an irrepressible audacity, an irresistible desire to conquer, which intense vitality often brings with it.'

That brings us a little nearer the ferocity of our own game, in which the commitment to winning is paramount. But Bloomer was hardly showered with reward. He got 7s 6d a week in his first season in the League in 1893.

Money became a vital influence on developments in football as soon as families realized that football could pay regular working wages. This was the point at which the game took on its widest significance. The growth of football is not a footnote to the social history of the twentieth century but a plain thread in it.

By the 1920s football was an established employer in a community where jobs were scarce. The clubs had grown up out of pride in athleticism, in local importance, in corporate endeavour. The stadiums were planted where the supporters lived, in among the industrial mazes of factories and hunched, workers' houses. The Saturday match became more than mere diversion from the daily grind, because there was often no work to be relieved. To go to the match was to escape from the dark of despondency into the light of combat. Here, by association with the home team, positive identity could be claimed by muscle and in goals. To win was personal success, to lose another clout from life. Football was not so much an opiate of the people as a flag run up against the gaffer bolting his gates and the landlord armed with his bailiffs.

The footballer as representative had become the true working-class hero. He came from these streets where the spectators lived. The spring grass and the winter mud on the other side of the stadium wall were within walking distance from where he played, kicking at makeshift balls, perhaps just bindings of rags, against doorways for goals. There was an urgency in this backstreet football that Eton and Charterhouse had never known. It had nothing to do with indolent elegance and taking hard knocks with stoical good grace. When there was no work to be had, and only the drudging kind when it was available, there was just a chance that a big lad could scrape into the police force; but suppose, God be good to us, he could make a footballer.

The pickings for professional players were meagre by the standards of the 1960s. By the mid-1930s a First Division player could not expect to take home more than £12 a week, even with his bonuses for playing in the senior side and for winning a match; a young player, to take the case of Stan Cullis, who joined Wolverhampton Wanderers in 1934, would get a basic wage of £2 10s to £3 in his first two seasons with his club. But there could be material extras, such as a free house for a married man and travel and hotel stops about the country; the local stature the job settled on the man was immense. He had moved out of the rigid oppressiveness of his class through his gifts in the people's art. The essence of the people's obsession with football was that it was far, far better than work. That thought will recur frequently in this book.

Cullis, who is now Birmingham City's manager, will figure at greater length in a chapter on managers, but his experience as a player entering professional football five years before the Second World War are relevant here, and illuminating. He was born at Ellesmere Port, near Liverpool, the youngest of ten children, but his father was a Wolverhampton man and when scouts from various League clubs approached him about Stan he always answered: 'When I decide he is good enough to play professionally he'll go to one club and no other.' The club was, of course, Wolves and Mr Cullis took his son there when the boy was 17.

Cullis had wanted to be a journalist but had left school at 15 and was working in a grocery shop, taking further lessons at night school. He remembers being taken to see Wolves' manager, the legendary martinet Major Buckley, at his home. Buckley, he says, 'looked like a retired, well-to-do farmer, because he always wore plus-fours. He looked like a man of the soil. No one ever thought of calling him anything else but "Major". It was his rank in the First World War'.

The interview was short and staccato. Cullis says: 'He looked me up and down as I imagine a bloodstock owner would look at a racehorse. He said, "Stand up." He tapped me on the chest and said, "What have you got there?" I didn't know what he meant. I thought he must mean something about my clothes. He said, "Are you frightened?" I said, "What of?" He said, "Of getting hurt." I said, "No." That was all he said to me. He had some words with my father which I couldn't hear, and I was a professional footballer.'

The next conversation Cullis had with his manager was equally terse: 'He gave me a very strict instruction about what I had to do if I wanted to make a success of the job. This first homily was, "You listen to me because I am going to be the most important man in your life from now on." '

Cullis's similarity with the players of the sixties is close because he was precocious. He was in Wolves' senior side at 17½ and its captain at 19. When he was 22 he was not only England's centre-half but captain as well. Yet he was not paid the professionals' maximum wage of £8 in the winter months and £6 in the summer until his third season with the club. The atmosphere in the game was always tense and the manner of it never delicate. 'It was a time of the survival of the fittest,' he remembers. 'There was a feeling of great insecurity. If you didn't make the grade you were on the dole.'

In view of how much howling of outrage has been heard recently about bad temper and viciousness on the field it is interesting to note Cullis's memories of the football in the thirties and the forties. He says: 'It was more rugged. There was more physical contact. We always had what we called the Killers in the game, players who went deliberately over the ball to get the man. They were all known, and you took special precautions against them. The play was rougher and dirtier than it is now.'

This period had drama, and the huge and roaring crowds, and it had brilliance of performance. But off the field the footballer was commonly closer to austerity than to flamboyance. The tenor of the age did not permit bold indecorum by adolescents in public, and no skinny youths had Cullis's name painted across the backs of their jackets, and no voluptuous, 15-year-old courtesans from housing estates sent him letters in perfumed envelopes asking for a night out. Stanley Matthews, one of the best known young Englishmen in the world at that time, did not get that kind of attention either.

.   .   .   .   .

Matthews at 19 played his first match on England's right wing in 1934, the same season that Cullis entered football. He scored a goal, and then a hat-trick in another international match three years later, which is startling to anyone of my generation. We remember him as a slightly humped, stiff-looking figure, rather like a Meccano man, darting suddenly towards and away from transfixed defenders, the ball not kicked by his feet but nudged between them, deftly and gently like butter being chopped up by a two-pat grocer. Thinking of Matthews in action now I can always see his bent shape from behind and one or two bigger men waiting for the lunge in front of him; there is hardly ever a set of goal posts in this frame; Matthews always seemed a very long way away from goal, which was the mistaken impression which deceived countless defenders when they thought there would be time for a second tackle if the first one missed. The ball would be curling into the stride of another forward in the penalty area before the fullback had got off his backside.

It is argued now that Matthews would have failed in modern football because of his limited specialization, because he never tackled an opposition forward or assisted in any sense in his own side's defensive pattern, because he would have been smacked hard to the ground by today's much faster, lighter, more tenacious defenders. We are never going to know the truth of this. I question it, not just because I dislike having my boyhood heroes squashed like trodden-on plasticine, but because I think people confuse Matthews's unique talent with all the lesser examples of the genre.

Matthews did not invent dribbling with a football; he raised it to its highest degree. Lots of other players did the same kind of thing at a lower level before him and throughout his career. Until George Best's arrival dribbling had been dead for nearly a decade for every player except Matthews and Bryan Douglas, of Blackburn Rovers, for any purposes except brief hiding of the ball from the opposition. It is now being restored to the game, accepted grudgingly by the managers again as a player's last resort against the sophistication of the retreating, blocking defensive technique. Running with a football, deliberately showing it to the opposition to force a tackle so that the defender can be eliminated, is such a knife-edge matter that a player hardly dares to fail. It needs extreme talent. It went out of favour, taking with it the reputation of the man who was best at it, because it lacked performers of sufficient quality. It always had, of course; but now defences were nimbler and could snuff out the second-grade ball-players at first stride.

It is endlessly beguiling to consider who was the greatest player in this position or that, and to wallow in that marvellous game, which alone made those school revision periods bearable, of picking the team called the International All-Time Greats. I would have the 35-year-old Matthews on my right wing and Best at inside-right and invite the opposition to find the ball.

Matthews was undeniably one of the phenomena of the game. His longevity of action in it alone sets him apart from any other player. His story is in the classic mould of the local urchin becoming golden boy. He was the son of a Hanley barber, a schoolboy international player, then an office boy at the Stoke City club when he was 14, becoming a professional player three years later. There were twenty-three years between his first game for England and his last. When he was about to leave Stoke City in 1938 there was a public protest meeting attended by 3,000 people. He moved to the Blackpool club in 1946, to collect a Cup winner's medal from an extraordinarily emotional Final when he was 38. Then he went back to Stoke in his declining years to help the club back up into the First

Division. In 1967, at 52 and manager of Port Vale, he was still turning out in friendly matches.

The self-discipline involved in regular training always meant much to Matthews. 'Fitness is confidence,' he said to me, when I talked to him at his home in Blackpool in 1965, just before he became a knight. He was still on Stoke's books as a player, although injury had kept him out of the team for weeks, and he was following an unbroken daily routine to keep himself brisk and supple. It did not vary whatever the weather or the time of year. He would get up at daylight, drink a cup of tea and drive to the beach; there he would breathe deep, do stretching exercises and sprint, a thin and angular figure well wrapped up and self-absorbed. All this might take half an hour or one and a half, according to how soon his body's responses told him he had done enough. Then he would drive home, take a cold shower and eat a breakfast of cereal, toast and honey. An old friend of his told me he once said to Matthews on some grisly, sleeting morning: 'You can't be serious about going training in this lot.' Matthews said simply: 'It's my living.'

It is complained that the Matthews life had veered from that of the dedicated footballer into something grotesquely compulsive, like a circus act preserved into aged ponderousness; that his last seasons at Stoke were a form of emotional black-mail both of the club's supporters and of the opposing defenders. The answer is the same answer that must be given to those who question his greatness even as a young player; whatever name you care to give it the Matthews act worked. The crowds had returned to Stoke, and the side had returned to Division One. He had compelled attention, which was very often his principal value when he was playing for England. It did not matter, least of all to Matthews, which of his side put the ball in the net. Football is not just a game.

In a sense Matthews's clinging to his playing days was very like the manner in which he played an individual match. When he moved with the ball, shuffling, leaning, edging ever closer to the defender, he was always the man teetering to the very brink of disaster, and we waited breathlessly to see whether this time he would fail or whether yet again he would come swaying back at the last possible moment to run on clear and free. This was how his career was for years. Could he carry on past 40? He played for his country at 42. Every season afterwards had to be his last. Or just one more? Would this be the very last game? Back he came for another. There was the courage of manhood here, of the very English, stubborn, contrary, self-determining kind.

Is Matthews, then, our immediate contact between yesterday's footballers and today's? The virtuosity was dazzling enough and the commitment to the business complete. But what did he get directly out of the game? His fanmail was always substantial, almost wholly from small boys and fathers. The children wanted his picture and his signature; the parents often wanted him to coach their sons privately, convinced that it needed only the touch of the master to transform the child into the genius. But the response he drew from the crowds was very different from the one Best gets. I think, for one thing, we were always afraid for Matthews, the non-athlete; the sadly impassive face, with its high cheekbones, pale lips and hooded eyes, had a lot of pain in it, the deep hurt that came from prolonged effort and the certainty of more blows. It was a worker's face, like a miner's, never really young, tight against a brutal world even in repose. We admired him deeply, urging him on but afraid for him too as he trotted up yet again to show his shins to a big young fullback and invite the lad to make a name for himself by chopping the old Merlin down.

The anxiety showed in Matthews too: again like the frail miner's fear of the job which must always be done, not joyfully but in deeper satisfaction, for self-respect. As Matthews said: 'It's my living.'

In communicating this frailty and this effort Matthews went to men's hearts, essentially to inconspicuous, mild working men's. He was the opposite of glamorous: a non-drinker, non-smoker, careful with his money. He had an habitual little cough. He was a representative of his age and his class, brought up among thrift and the ever-looming threat of dole and debt. For as long as he was one of the world's fleetest movers he never had exuberance. He came from that England which had no reason to know that the twenties were Naughty and the thirties had Style.

His name was shouted a lot in unison, the two syllables lending themselves to a most satisfying sound. With England's team abroad, particularly, the sound registered hauntingly in other players' minds: 'Ma-*tooz*, Ma-*tooz*.' Materially he made the kind of living that could be expected by an enterprising provincial businessman with shops in two or three High streets and no time for frivolous spending. He always said that while his fame came from football very little of his money did; he has had years of royalties from the use of his name in advertising football boots and health food, he wrote two autobiographies and a column for the *Sunday Express*, and for several years he ran a hotel in Blackpool. His home in the town in 1965 was a big, family house with a tennis court in the back garden. It was furnished and warmed for the comfort of a finicky, well-off, middle-aged man anxious about draughts; in the mid-after-noons he and his wife would eat a seemly tea in the sitting-room, after Matthews had taken the telephone off the hook. When he dealt with his mail afterwards there were usually letters from men his own age reminding him of games they saw him play when they were both twenty.

He is not a good talker, and smiles come sparingly from him. The overriding impression he gave in his home was of acute, conscious wariness, just as on the football field. He said that throughout his career he always had severe nausea in the dressing-room before a match, and then one could understand why his face was not an expression of arrested youth to match the lightness of his movements.

But while he was no conversational song-and-dance man he was careful not to be trite. Considering the game as he heard it discussed by other people, he said: 'Well, when some of these youngsters start telling you they beat one man, then two men, then three men, well I don't know what they're talking about. I never know whether I've beaten one man or three or four. It's just feet.'

He thought then he would continue for three or four years more as an exhibition player, touring abroad as he had almost every summer since 1946. But soon afterwards he took on the management of Port Vale, slumped in Division Four. When I went to see him there in 1967 he was committed to a policy of trying to build a new club around a frame of principally teenage players. Any Fourth Division club is at a disadvantage in the competition for likely youngsters' signatures because the glamour of the First Division is so alluring. Matthews was travelling a great deal, visiting parents, his name and his face still counting for much. He said: 'I tell them that they can hold me personally responsible for seeing that their boys are well looked after.'

Some weeks after this meeting Matthews was in serious trouble over the club's dealings with young players. A joint FA and League committee found Port Vale guilty of paying wages to schoolboys and to registered amateurs, and also of offering illegal bonuses to players. In March 1968, the League expelled the club for these offences, as from the end of the season. (At its annual general meeting the League voted to readmit Port Vale to Division Four for the 1968–9 season; but Sir Stanley resigned.) There is a further comment in the final chapter.

Matthews was still physically unmistakable as the spare man with the slanted eyes I knew first of all from the portrait cards which used to come with my father's cigarettes. He ate salad and crispbread for lunch, and he was wearing houndstooth check trousers, a black blazer and a milk-white, polo-neck pullover. He said that ninety minutes of a friendly football match gave him no distress, and he sounded well pleased about it. 'If I don't train it won't affect me in the game,' he said. 'But it hurts more the next day.'

I have never heard anyone talking about football in the 1940s and 1950s who captures the flavour of the period more convincingly than Nat Lofthouse, the Bolton centre-forward who played thirty-three times for England. He was built in the manner required for the times, with a navvy's forearms and shoulders and a special darkness of expression when he was playing which reflected his intention of single-minded antagonism for the other team's defenders. He was described in print when a player both as 'a bear' and 'a lion', and certainly any sportswriter looking for a suitable comparison in the animal world would have to keep clear of the antelope department. It was for the exploitation of ferocious goal-scorers like Lofthouse, central to the objective in football, that the kind of skills perfected by Matthews were developed in the first place.

Lofthouse was born in Bolton, the son of a coal-bagger – that is, for readers outside the northern, heavy industrial scene, a

man who humped sacks of coal to householders' backyards off
his horse-drawn cart. The first representative match of any
kind he experienced was when he played for his school at the
age of 11. 'They were a man short, so they put me in goal. I
was only there because I'd gone to watch my brother play. I
remember it because I had on a new pair of shoes. Brand new,
they were, and I kicked hell out of 'em.'

This game was a revelation to the boy, because until then
the only football he knew at first hand, outside the familiar but
vaguely understood talk about Bolton Wanderers, was the kind
played on greasy stretches of waste ground, when there might
be six players to a side or twenty. Lofthouse remembered: 'If
you got kicked on the leg you just waited until the next time
you saw the bloke and kicked him back.' These were not games
confined entirely to boys of Lofthouse's age. They were those
fierce shouting and swearing affairs known to anyone brought
up in such an area, which would cover an age range from about
10 to anywhere around 30; television may have reduced the
incidence of this kind of football nowadays, but up to the early
1950s they were the common self-entertainment of the spring
and autumn evenings between teatime and moonlight.

But this first game under authoritative management introduced a new dimension. Lofthouse recalled his surprise: 'There
was a bloke in the middle controlling it. He was the referee,
but I'd never seen one before. I thought, "Well, this is easier."
I could see what the game was about.' He asked his teacher for
a regular game for his school, and was made centre-forward.
'There was no reason for it then. It was just that I was always
a big lad.' Then he started 'pinching in' (sneaking up the
drainpipe) at Bolton Wanderers' ground to see League matches.

He began to arouse local interest as a player in a youth side
when he was appreciably younger than most of the other

B

players. One day at school a Wanderers' director, Alderman
Entwhistle, then the Mayor of Bolton, no less, astonished Lofthouse by asking him if he would like to play for the club. 'I
went home and told me dad. I thought it must be a joke or
something. But Bolton contacted us soon afterwards, and I
signed for the club when I was 14.'

The boy's euphoria ended abruptly. This was 1939 and in
that ominous autumn when Hitler was hogging the front pages.
Lofthouse said: 'As I walked through the gates of Burnden Park
(Bolton Wanderers' ground) all the players were lining up in
rows on the field. They were disbanding. It was the war.' He
had been taken on the ground staff, but instead he was found
a job somewhere else in the town and put on Bolton's books as
an amateur player. By the time he was 15 he was playing in the
makeshift first team, under the wartime arrangements which
allowed for guest players borrowed from whatever Forces units
were at hand. Lofthouse found himself playing with men like
Tom Finney, unarguably already one of the great players of all
time, and Bill Shankly, now Liverpool's manager.

'This was really something,' Lofthouse said, and even nearly
thirty years later, a man in his 40s with a son at university and
a teenage daughter, he conveyed spontaneously the boy's sense
of wonder and high privilege. 'I was playing with people I'd
only ever seen before a hundred yards away when I was
standing on an embankment. And people were *paying* to watch
me.' He chewed on that memory for a while, and then said:
'They were very patient. When I think about it now I was very
limited.'

Initially he was paid expenses of 2s 6d a week, then 3s 6d,
then 7s 6d. When he signed for the club as a professional at 17
his pay was £1 10s a week.

Lofthouse weighed 12 stone 2 lb. when he was 15, and four

years in the coal pits as a Bevin Boy, the wartime conscription alternative to military service, helped to harden him in his attitude to life as well as in his muscle. His early coaching in football had been elementary by the standards of schoolboy training today, and he had to develop his skills largely on his own initiative. He always had that compulsion which is special to many a born centre-forward to strike the ball with his head rather than his feet. 'I always felt more *confident* if I could jump up at the ball than if I had it at my feet.' He spent hours heading a tennis ball against a wall at home. But his lack of specialized coaching showed in his game as a young player, and he struggled through a long period of derision from Bolton's supporters and colder criticism from the newspapers. Both kinds of attention hurt. 'I always liked to see my name in the paper.'

Fortune changed for him suddenly, and when he considers the change he says frankly that he cannot connect it with any devotion to training or any conscious switch of method on his part. 'You just don't know how it comes. You could say your luck turns. Just like that. One day you go up for a ball and, bang, it's in the net. You've been doing the same thing for months and getting nothing for it. That's how it was. No one was more surprised than me.'

Whether it was good luck or reward for persistence the change at last justified Bolton in their perseverance with the home-grown coalman's boy. Personal success brought Lofthouse a new assurance in his strength and his capacity to outjump, out-muscle, outlast most of the League's centre-halves. He became a specialist in scoring with headers from corner kicks, a centre-forward's ploy rendered less menacing in the game nowadays by the extra agility and anticipative intelligence of defences. 'I used to be pretty certain that I'd at least get a touch to the ball.

And the moment I hit it I always knew when it was going in. I think most players do. It's a great feeling.'

It was especially pleasing to a player who had been dispirited by lack of success to the point of seriously considering giving up the game at 19. This was the centre-forward who made a reality of that ambition so immense that even heroes in boys' adventure fiction are seldom allowed it: he scored a hat-trick in each half of the same match, playing for the English League against the League of Ireland on Wolverhampton Wanderers' ground.

Lofthouse likes to talk about that match, not just because he scored six times in it but also because he enjoys telling the story of 'the only time I ever heard Alf Ramsey booed'. Ramsey, now England's international team manager, was captain of the side, and it had been agreed that any penalty kicks should be taken by him. When a penalty was awarded – 'I got it,' Lofthouse says, making the point that penalties are not always calamities which happen, negatively, to the offending side without any intentional contribution by the man fouled – the crowd roared Lofthouse's name. 'But the captain picked the ball up and put it on the spot. That was when he was booed. I must say that Alf did ask me, and I said, "No, let's stick to what we said." I never took a single penalty as a professional footballer.'

Lofthouse made a telling point about the difference between playing, however spectacularly, with second-grade players and being in a side with virtuosos. He said: 'With Matthews and Finney you knew that if you gave them the ball they'd either beat a man and get a cross over to you or they'd manage somehow to give you the ball back. They'd always do *something*. They wouldn't just lose the thing. The worst thing that can happen to a centre-forward is to get no support.

If the ball's just banged away anywhere by the defence that's demoralizing.'

The immediate financial reward was paltry by today's standards. His basic weekly wage rose to £12, then to £14, to £17, and then by the late 1950s to the maximum the League would allow, £20. But there were substantial extras for putting his name to newspaper articles, for a book, for appearances on television and for making personal appearances at the opening of new shops. For some time he was the testimonial to the health-giving value of Andrews' Liver Salts. He said: 'Well, all right, so I had to sit there for an hour while they took the pictures. I was getting *paid* for that.'

He travelled with football teams all over Europe, to South America, to the West Indies, to the USA and to Canada, and when he came home to Bolton from any of these trips he was conscious of his local importance, of the glitter dust of glamour that shone on him as it shines on any distant traveller when he returns to the streets where there is no horizon beyond the foreman's job and the spray obscuring Blackpool's foreshore.

For a while he was landlord of a pub, where he both enjoyed the avidity of the regulars for his stories and felt the duty in his privilege of telling them. 'I'd be in the vault when these lads would come in on their way home from work for a couple of pints before their tea. They'd be asking me all about it, what it was like in Argentina, what did I eat in Trinidad. I'd be talking to them, telling them what I could remember, and they'd be listening to me, every word. I got a kick out of it. I used to say to myself, "By God, there's a bloke here, he's never been out of Bolton." I was giving them pleasure. They'd be saying, "By the 'eck, gerraway, yer don't mean it." And I'd been paid for all this, *well* paid to them. You could say I'd only been getting 14 quid a week, but it wasn't really work. They were working damned hard for 8 quid. I got easy money. I know; I've worked down the pit and I've played football.'

Lofthouse, now Bolton's chief coach, a vigorous, friendly man with a snappy sports saloon outside his house, caught the essential gratitude and surprise of the working man that worldly comfort can be his without the drudgery of manual labour. It is one of the key factors in the people's embrace and nurturing of football.

Lofthouse had stopped playing before he had time to benefit from the abolition of the maximum wage for footballers in 1961, so that while he achieved comfort and a degree of wealth which he knows would probably have been beyond his reach but for his ability to head goals, he never could have matched the careless flourish of affluence that came to young footballers in the sixties. Yet, as a young player in the years of social liberation after the Second World War, he could give rein to his relish for the spotlight and the modest fruits of the game. Because he was a star footballer he was fortunate: he told his neighbours so and they liked him the more for it. Such a hero is appointed by the people, not by any manipulators, and one of his duties is to show that he's got it good. They like him to enjoy himself on their behalf, just as he scores goals for them. Lofthouse, so different a player from George Best, was close to Best's attitude to the game and matched his delight in the success it brought him. The more articulate of the two, Lofthouse said just what Best indicated about his own moments of sweetness when he talked about one memorable early morning in Bolton:

'The team was going to South Africa free for nine weeks. I'd left my house at half past seven to be picked up by the coach

at the bottom of the road. There's a works down there and the
men were all rolling in. Half past *seven*, that was, and I was
there with my cases going to South Africa for nine weeks, all
paid with £2 a day spending money.' Lofthouse conveyed a
sense of victory, not just pleasure, when he said that.

The years 1960 to 1963 were of crucial importance to British
football. They marked the end of the total dominance of the
game's boardrooms over the players. It was an extraordinary
anomaly that although the professional player had for eighty
years decided the nature and manner of his sport only now did
he cease to be the voiceless chattel of its management.

Two events, the first in 1961 and the second two years later,
brought the change. First came the abolition of the League's
stipulation of a maximum player's wage; then came the High
Court judgement in the case of EASTHAM versus NEWCASTLE
UNITED FOOTBALL CLUB LTD AND OTHERS, which declared
the League's system of retain and transfer of players to be an
unjustifiable restraint of trade. The effect of these two events
was to make every professional player a free agent, just like a
journalist or an insurance salesman, able to negotiate his pay
and his length of service with a club, subject only to the kind
of contractual conditions which protect employer and employed
against unreasonableness from each other. It sounds a proper
and normal enough situation now, but it needed the threat of
a strike and George Eastham's stubborn insistence on justice
to bring it about.

Let's look at the question of wages first. As I have shown
already, the money paid in salaries to professional footballers
right up to the end of the 1950s was derisive in comparison
with what could be earned by entertainers performing in front
of much smaller audiences in, say, the theatre or cabaret. The

Football League had always laid down the maximum rates which could be paid to players, and in 1960 the figures were £20 during the playing months and £17 in the summer close season. But whereas smaller sums paid before the war had kept professional footballers generally up alongside the skilled workers of industry – and well ahead of the unskilled, to say nothing of the legion of unemployed – a wage like this was small beer to what could be earned on the production lines of some of the country's post-war, streamlined factories.

There were extra payments, but again strictly laid down by the League. Talent money could be paid on the following basis: at the end of the season £1,000 to be shared among all the players who had made first team appearances for the club at the top of the First Division and the one at the top of the Second; £880 to be distributed among the runners-up; £660 to be shared among those in third position; the club winning Division Three could share out £550 among its players; the Division Four champions could share out £330.

More immediate payments for week-by-week incentives were confined to £4 for a win in a League match and £2 for a draw, and in the FA Cup competition ranged from £4 for a win in Round One to £25 for winning the Final. These were stipu-lated sums. Clubs were *permitted* to distribute £1,100 among the team if it won the Cup and £880 if it lost in the Final. A team could get a bonus of £50 a man for winning the European Cup.

Taking these figures, what was the situation at its best for a leading professional footballer? Even in the unlikely event of his being in the team which won the League championship and the FA Cup and got as far as the final tie of the European Cup his pay from his club would not legally rise above £1,500 for the year. Even with a free house and a good deal of first-class travel about Britain and the Continent this hardly added up to a position of affluent abandon.

Quite plainly, it was not enough. The players knew it and so did the clubs. The consequence was that for years under-the-counter payments were made to players. They were whispered, denied, confessed, denied again. But they were irregular in more senses than one, and many leading players thought themselves obliged to cash in on their fame by taking jobs outside football to boost their assured incomes. They became car salesmen, typewriter salesmen, holiday salesmen. The jobs were not sinecures; the value of the players lay in their physical presence alongside the firms' wares.

At its least damaging this kind of position lacked dignity, because the player and the public knew very well that the man was in the job because he was a good advertisement and not because he knew much about cars or space bars. The more famous the player the more undignified the job; it is one thing to have your face smiling healthily from an advertising hoarding and another to appeal personally to fans to buy Bloggs's goods not for Bloggs's sake but your own. Many other players tried to avoid this situation by borrowing money on their names and setting up small enterprises, such as sweetshops and women's hairdressing businesses, for their wives to run. In either case the outside work reduced the commitment of their minds and energies to football.

The footballer knew well enough that his life in the game was limited. If he was playing League football by the time he was 18 or 19 he could not expect to stay in the game, except in the rarest cases, after 35; the chance of becoming a manager, coach or trainer after his playing days were over was not high, because there are far more players than professional clubs. Cliff Lloyd, the secretary of the Professional Footballers Association, the players' union, put this situation succinctly for me. He was first a halfback, then a fullback, and he played with Liverpool, Fulham, Wrexham and Bristol Rovers, and he said that there came a point after which he dreaded birthdays. 'I knew,' he said, 'that it was just one year nearer the time when I would have to retire.'

That fear was not just the deepening regret that comes to men who know that youth is receding and the pleasure and excitement of athleticism are going with it; it was the knowledge that a new way of earning a living would have to be found at a time when most specially talented men in other fields are still below the peak of their careers.

The PFA had always worried at this problem, but in 1960 they attacked it dramatically. Their chairman was Jimmy Hill (then playing with Fulham and later an innovating manager of Coventry) and his leadership was impressive. He had always at his shoulder Cliff Lloyd, a stocky, wary, well-informed blocker of the opposition and prompter of assault, fittingly for an ex-fullback, and behind him a firm of solicitors solidly in support of the players' case, for more than professional reasons. The cause was just, and no amount of feigned moral outrage or prophecy of disaster by some of the clubs' directors could make it look otherwise.

I remember one of the players' meetings at Belle Vue, Manchester, when the Press were invited to sit in on the voting for strike action. There was always a certain amount of private ridicule among the groups of reporters covering this prolonged story; the impression of professional footballers as neolithic mumblers with their hands held out palms upwards never had much substance, but its suggestible, comic qualities had persuaded credence in some quarters. The air was blue with cigarette smoke, and we nudged each other indignantly about that; but Hill surprised us with his very quotable lucidity, and the players voted to a man to strike unless they got satisfaction. The meeting was serious, bitter, orderly.

In the middle of the 1960–61 season the PFA issued their strike notice. They asked for the abolition of maximum wage, and for the introduction of three-year contracts for players. In January of 1961, three days before the strike notice was due to expire, the League capitulated on the question of the maximum wage and, apparently – but only apparently – accepted the principle that the old retain and transfer system had to go.

The clubs' directors, as a group, have to be heavily censured, as they were at the time by several newspapers, for their failure to turn that apparent agreement into practice. Some months afterwards the League, at its annual general meeting, decided that the retain and transfer system would still be applied. They were defeated in the end in the most effective way possible – in the High Court, and over the case of a footballer whose personal dispute with his club, the matter which led to the action in the first place, had by then been settled. There was justice in the irony.

George Eastham, the player concerned, had found himself in a position common to many footballers. He was a brilliantly gifted forward, of the thoughtful kind whom the game calls a 'schemer'; he was an England international. He was the key figure in Newcastle United's forward line, but he and the club management fell out and he asked for a transfer. The club declined to give him one, put him on its list of retained players at his old wage and that, as far as the rules of the League went, was that. The iniquity of the retain and transfer system was that the clubs were wholly in control. If Newcastle had decided to pay him only the minimum wage of £8 a week Eastham would have been forced to stay with them unless he could persuade the League Management Committee to intervene under an appeals rule.

He appealed and the Management Committee decided it had no cause to intervene. The acrimony between the player and Newcastle's management developed. Eastham did not play football for a year. Backed by the PFA he began the legal action which eventually freed all players from a system described by Eastham's counsel in the trial as being like the bartering of cattle and a relic of the Middle Ages.

Long before the case came before Mr Justice Wilberforce Eastham was not much more of an interested party, except in terms of moral satisfaction, than any other professional player; he had been at last transferred by Newcastle to Arsenal. The situation freed this celebrated case from most of the personal animosity present when proceedings were first begun; its extra clinicality gave it extra point.

Eastham claimed a declaration against Newcastle United, against its six directors and its manager, and against the Football League and the Football Association that the regulations which had prevented his transfer from Newcastle were an unreasonable restraint of his trade. The judgement was delivered on July 4, 1963. Eastham won.

What came out in the trial, as far as the League and Newcastle's directors were concerned, was primarily the fear that to allow players to have too great a say in how much they should be paid and for whom they should work would open professional football to anarchy. The suggestion seemed to be that to give the players the whiphand would be to turn the professional game into a chaos of grabbing for the fruits; the rich clubs would collar all the best players, the poorer ones would go to the wall.

What this thinking more widely suggested was a deep

cynicism among the controllers of football about the motives
of players, and it went very ill with the image many clubs'
directors liked to offer of wise avuncularity, encouraging and
coaxing young athletes into more effort for the entertainment
of the populace and for its greater civic pride.

But the process of the running down of small clubs in the
Third and Fourth Divisions had already begun, not because
players wanted more money but because a more mobile, more
amused population was ready and able to travel further for its
enjoyment. The leading teams certainly have spent massively
on buying other clubs' players, but the most successful of them
at the time of writing are those which have concentrated most
on building teams out of home-trained players, or those bought
very young, and then *keeping* them by imaginative and generous
treatment. The key point which applied before the Eastham
case and still applies now is that the compulsion of football
creates players and drives them before anything else. The
PFA's campaign was essentially for greater freedom for the
player to follow his game, not just for more money for good
players and more security for lesser ones.

Cliff Lloyd said to me in 1967, four years after the historic
court case, that he was convinced no other events in football
had done more to lift the general standard of play to its present
high level than these two. What is more, he said that he always
maintained England could win the 1966 World Cup (as she
did) if her players were liberated from the restrictions binding
them so unreasonably, and in so much resentment, to clubs
and low rewards. He said, with cold and telling perception,
that without this liberation football would have gradually
dwindled to the same sad status that county cricket has in
England – 'a jolly day out, take-it-or-leave-it sort of thing'.

I, for one, could not bear my football to look like that.

3 The Inheritors

For some of the star performers in football the 'new deal' has
clearly meant an everyday life transformed from the kind led
by the previous generation. The rewards for successful football
are now more nearly commensurate with the players' positions
as vastly popular entertainers. A leading player, negotiating his
pay and his bonuses with his club, can now assure himself a
basic salary of perhaps £3,500 to £5,000 a year, and his incen-
tive bonuses are far in excess of the end-of-term prizes the clubs
used to hand out.

Bonuses for winning individual matches are still pegged by
the regulations at £4 for a win and £2 for a draw in League
matches and still range from £4 to £25 as a team makes progress through the FA Cup rounds. But the clubs get round this
obstacle by writing into players' contracts bonuses for achieving
certain objectives at various stages of the season. A player's
contract may say that if after the first ten League matches the
team has won more than 18 points there will be a share-out of
perhaps £2,000 among the side; or if the team has won more
than 15 points a share-out of perhaps £1,500. The contract
can also provide that later in the season, when success or failure
is becoming more vital, the bonus may be for as much as £4,000
for the team if it is at the top of the table after a certain number
of games. The same side may share half that figure for lying
third at this stage. For winning the championship of the
Division the bonus may be £1,000 a man.

In the Cup rounds the bonuses can be more for some players
than used to be paid to a man throughout the season before
1961. These bonuses may not be uniform throughout the side.
A star player may have in his contract a promise of a £3,000

bonus if the club wins the Cup, or half that if it reaches the final. More usually, though, the bonus offered will be the same for the whole team.

There are further bonuses paid to players as reward for bringing the crowds in. Many of the leading clubs, instead of giving incentives for winning a run of games, pay their first team £1 or £2 a player for every 1,000 spectators in any given home crowd which exceeds a certain number – usually around the 25,000, 30,000 or 35,000 mark, according to what size of crowd the club can expect even in thin times. They may pay the same bonus the following week, when the team plays away. These attendance bonuses are also common among the smaller clubs, beginning with crowds of perhaps 8–10,000.

These extra payments add up to big pay. It is clear that a handful of the leading players, perhaps a dozen or twenty men in the successful teams, are collecting sums of £10,000 or £12,000 for a year's football. This does not include what income may be theirs from advertising contracts or from businesses they may set up under their names for managers to run.

Yet, while this sort of money sounds startling in Britain when applied to footballers, such sums do not surprise Italians or South Americans when they discuss football and cash. For years before the maximum wage was abolished in Britain the star players in Italy, Portugal, Spain, Brazil, the Argentine, were rewarded like pop singers or film stars. And even if we say that £10,000 or £12,000 a year is big money for a man to earn in his 20s it must be remembered that he can manage it only in the few years in which he can stay right at the top. Young, lithe, theatre Romeos can grow up into grizzled, resonant Lears and still make a fortune; there are no 45-year-old centre-forwards in the FA Cup Final.

This is not to say, in any case, that earnings on this scale apply commonly even in the First Division of the Football League. Given that less successful clubs attract fewer people, win fewer points, make less progress in knock-out competitions, the players' pay comes down sharply from these top figures. In the middle and lower reaches of Division One earnings are as often under as over £3,000 a year, in Division Two often under £2,000; in the Third and Fourth Divisions, while the ambitious clubs with energetic public relations measures which bring in the crowds may match Second Division wages, generally the weekly pay is about that of a semi-skilled worker on overtime or a senior clerk in industry. But there are often free houses.

One of the important results of the PFA's campaign for a 'new deal' has been that players are now entitled to a percentage of any transfer fees paid for them by one club to another. Previously a man could claim, legally, £20 as a signing-on bonus from his new club. Now there is a 10 per cent levy on the fee, half of which goes to the League to augment a provident fund for lower-paid players, and half to the player, although if the man is transferred at his own request and not at that of his old club he gets his 5 per cent only if he satisfies the League Management Committee that his request to move was made 'on reasonable grounds'. Now that transfer fees of £50,000 and more are commonplace it matters greatly to a player that he should not appear unreasonable in his dissatisfaction with the club he wants to leave. No one wants to lose £2,500 just for being truculent.

The essential general point which emerges from these facts is that football is now, more than ever it was, a source of good jobs, at least in a man's young years.

When Everton beat Sheffield Wednesday 3–2 in the FA Cup

Final in 1966 Sheffield's centre-half was a tall, big-shouldered 19-year-old with red hair, whose previous experience in top quality football amounted to six matches in his club's first team. Sam Ellis had left school at 17 with ten passes at Ordinary level in his GCE, and Advanced levels in economics, history and geography, and he chose to be a professional footballer in preference to going on to University to take a central government course.

Ellis is a representative of the new breed of professional player which is going to be more and more common in the game in the coming years. For a youth of his educational capacities it is not enough that the game can give him a job; it has to be attractive beyond the security and status of the civil service or the bank. That is what sets him apart from the generations which needed to play football to avoid the pit or the dole.

He is an easy, casual talker, pleased at occasional dramatic impact on the listener. His grounding in the game was the same in essence as Nat Lofthouse's twenty years earlier. He was a football fan's son, and at his junior school he played for the area boys' team for his age group. But he then found himself at Audenshaw Grammar School, in North Manchester, which played rugby. 'Not football at all,' Ellis said, sounding in 1967 as offended as he must have been when he first encountered the fact. He missed his football so much that he asked his father to form a youth team so that he could play.

'Dad didn't need much persuading,' Ellis recalled. The team was composed mostly of Ellis's immediate friends, several of them out of his own class at school, and it stayed together for three seasons in the same local league, winning it once, being runners-up once and winning its knock-out cup competition. 'The field we played in was next door to our house, right next to the garden, and the opposing teams used to change in our house. I played for other teams, as well. I'd go anywhere for a game. I'd play in goal if that was all I could get.'

These were mostly Saturday morning games. On Saturday afternoons he went with his father, a railway traffic inspector, and quite often his younger sister as well, to watch Manchester City at Maine Road. 'We used to get there at half past one so that Dad could get me a safe place up against a barrier.'

In his mid-teens, being now adult size, he played for a while for a side in the Manchester Amateur League. When he was 17, 'a mad keen football fan' who lives in Altrincham but who used to live in Sheffield got him a trial at Sheffield Wednesday. The pace of this class of football astonished him. He said: 'When I was playing with the amateurs I used to think it was really fast, but after the trial I was stiff all over.' He had never seriously considered himself as a likely professional player, although, as he said, 'I'd imagined it a lot as a kid.' He had a trial week at Sheffield, played for the junior side against Huddersfield and gave away a penalty which allowed the opposition their goal in a 1–1 draw, and was then entirely surprised by being offered a job with the club.

He said: 'I'd stayed in a big hotel in Sheffield, and I'd never done that before. I'd met all the big players at the club. I just thought it had been a great experience, just something I'd have to remember all my life. To be honest, I thought I was too old to be taken on, because all the others were about 15, hoping to get in as apprentices.' He signed as a professional close to his 18th birthday in September 1964.

Ellis's sense of wonder at being a paid, full-time footballer was still with him after nearly two seasons of First Division matches, a lot of knocks, praise and substantial earnings. It is a sense which stays with many players throughout their careers

– even, or rather particularly, with some of the very best of them. For many players, as with fans, the game seems constantly to engage the imagination, to amaze with its drama, to sever the man from mundanity. Richard Hoggart, in *The Uses of Literacy*, has a deeply disturbing line about the drying up of the people's 'springs of assent', as they see the exploiter's greedy hand behind one after another of the excitements they have cherished. Football's innate truth of talent and conflict is what keeps it out of that discouraging, but true, generalization.

Ellis can remember the detail of his first weeks in first-class football exactly, and he gave me the impression that he always will. His first League match, in April 1966, was on a Monday night against Blackpool. This being the end of the season, the fixtures had piled up. He played again on Wednesday, and then on Saturday. Vic Mobley, the team's regular centre-half whom he had replaced because of an ankle injury, returned to the team for the match the following Wednesday. But Mobley's ankle was injured again when Sheffield beat Chelsea the next Saturday in the semi-final of the FA Cup. Ellis was back in the side.

Ellis said to me: 'To tell you the truth I never played really well in any of the six games I had before the Cup Final. I don't know what it was; I'd played better in the reserves. It wasn't that I was consciously thinking of playing in the Final. As far as I was concerned Vic had a fifty-fifty chance of playing at Wembley, and I was just pleased to be back in the first team. But the boss (Alan Brown, Sheffield Wednesday's manager at the time) kept telling me I was doing all right and that I had to keep going up for every ball and put the opposition off. The Thursday before Wembley he told me I was playing.'

The atmosphere at Wembley on Cup Final day is unique in football. It is more than just a great annual festival for the country which founded the game. It has much of the quality of remembrance because of its emotional association with old heroes and yesterday's triumphs and sadness. In this huge stadium 100,000 people are held in a communal passion, involved in a will to win so intense that it releases tears and fury even from those who elsewhere would permit neither except in the presence of extreme pain or violence. To be a foreigner at the Cup Final must be a strangely excluding experience. The British do not look like this in any other circumstances. When we stand and sing *Abide With Me*, maudlin and mindlessly fervent, we reach a state of sincere patriotism, sentimental beyond our beer and quite beyond even our own ridicule.

The nature of the high tension makes itself felt in advance. Anyone who cares at all about football wakes up jumpy on Cup Final day. Players discuss whether they were nervous or not during the Cup Final as soldiers discuss their first experience of battle and women their first labour.

Ellis said he felt perfectly normal before Wembley during the teams' interviews for television in the morning and while watching all the pre-match warm-up on the screen at the hotel. He said: 'It hit me when we walked out of the hotel to the coach. It was only ten yards. I felt my stomach go over, and then all I could feel was my stomach. I thought, "Ooh, what am I going to do?" It lasted twenty minutes. All I could think was, "What am I going to do?" It was terrible.' He said it was not until he was walking round the pitch with the rest of the team just before the match that he began to feel fully fit again. He played confidently and efficiently. It was a much more experienced player, making the elementary mistake of failing to deal decisively with an awkward bounce, who let an Everton player through to score the winning goal.

Ellis in 1967 was not earning £100 a week. He was only

slightly irritated, and not at all surprised, that people seemed to think all First Division players earned such a sum. He said he thought people liked to believe the myth because it gave them more justification for shouting from the terraces that they could do better themselves. He bought a modest car some months after the Cup Final. 'People thought I could have bought it with what I was paid for that match alone, but it wasn't true. I'd been saving up ever since I joined the club.'

He was living in digs with another player and several students at Sheffield University. After most Saturday matches he drove home to spend the weekend with his parents and to see his old friends and get ribbed about Sheffield Wednesday's fortunes as well as Manchester City's. During the week he listened to records a lot. If he went out on Thursday nights it would be to a cinema; he never went out on Friday nights. He found, moving about the town, that people wanted to talk to him about football. 'They're always saying, "Why don't you do this or that?" I just say, "yes" and "no". I never tell them they're talking a lot of bull, which they usually are.'

Because he is a big man, and as a centre-half is immediately regarded as one of the hard policemen of the game, he was troubled a little by local toughies who asked their critical questions aggressively, making the point that they were afraid of no overpaid footballer. He said: 'To be honest there are times when you'd like to find out just how tough some of these people are. But you can't afford to get involved in that sort of thing.'

His intelligence was plain. His fluency, with accurate verbs and a lucid rhythm in his talk, gave him a wry dignity for a very young man. He said he had looked into the possibility of taking an external university degree but had rejected the idea. It would take four years, which seemed an age, and he was afraid of anything which might detract from his football. For the same reason he had given no serious thought to starting a business outside football. 'I'm frightened of losing some of my game,' he said. 'I don't think I'm as good yet as I should be.' He had been concentrating, in extra training hours, on developing his heading of the ball.

Ellis, at 21, felt secure as a professional in football, but not complacent. He was still working for improvements in the game, watching it unravelling for him, enjoying it deeply and glad he was in it. His name was being shouted when he walked about the streets. He had seen Mexico and Bulgaria. He was unaffected in manner. The words which occurred most frequently in his conversation, the Manchester voice unmistakable, were 'me mum' and 'me dad'.

By 1967 a sprinkling of Eastern European names had occurred in the team lists of the Football League clubs, as the sons of some of the displaced families which arrived in Britain at the end of the Second World War began to make their mark on the English game. Sheffield Wednesday had three Nowakowski brothers, the sons of a Polish father and Ukrainian mother who arrived in Bradford in 1946. The eldest of the boys was Kazimierz, aged 19, known to the other Sheffield players as Kass and to the young fans who wrote letters to him as 'Mr Nov'. He was the left fullback for the reserves, and determined to play League football.

The story of his arrival in professional football had affecting and comic qualities, both heightened by his quiet, pointed delivery in what must have sounded in backstreet Bradford, where his parents still lived, as distinctly scholarly English. He and his brothers had to learn the language at school because they heard nothing but Polish at home. The lessons, Nowakowski said, were complemented by what was picked up in the rougher school of the streets and on the patches of open ground in the town where he and his brothers were introduced to football.

It was an austere childhood, their father struggling on a warehouseman's wage in a strange country. They lived in what Nowakowski carefully called 'a very poor district' right up against Valley Parade, the Bradford City (Division Four) ground. Their names, their language, their foreign connection, made the boys curiosities in a tightly knit, working-class community. The rough-house, spontaneous football of the streets was fiercely competitive. 'At school,' Nowakowski said, 'because we were strange we were always getting bullied and kicked around.' He was certain the experience toughened his and his brothers' resolve to get into professional football.

They were reared, as far as the professional game was concerned, on the matches at Valley Parade. He and Stanislaw, a year younger, and Zbigniew (renamed Bezek locally), three years younger, talked of little else but football as small boys, and littered the house with photographs of players. The passion was entirely lost on their father, whose main concern was that his eldest son should pursue his education and make a place for himself in the world as an interpreter. Kazimierz's prime interest was in getting a place in the school football team.

He had a stiff problem. He was good enough but was kept out of the Saturday morning matches because of his father's insistence that he went to a special session of a Polish school opened on Saturdays for families like the Nowakowskis. Kazimierz got round the obstacle for six months by writing letters in Polish, purporting to come from his father, saying that he had TB. He said: 'Every Saturday morning I used to walk out of the house with my books, leave them behind the

dustbin and pick up my football boots.' It worked long enough
to see him over to grammar school. There his talent as a player
was too marked to be ignored by anyone, and he played
regularly for the school team, at various age groups, right
through the school. He captained the Bradford Boys under-15
side, played for a West Riding county boys team and was
substitute for an English grammar schools side. His two brothers
were already on Sheffield Wednesday's books, Stanislaw as a
professional, Zbigniew as an apprentice, when he signed
professional forms for the club in the summer, near his 19th
birthday. His father was still opposed to his being a footballer.
Kazimierz decided for himself. He said in his soft, deliberate
voice: 'I was determined to make it.'

The hard and uncertain childhood had left its imprint,
although not physically; he was a strong-looking, assured youth,
with a neat haircut, a grey suit with a waistcoat and a composed handsomeness. The hardness was below the surface. He
was making sure of substantial educational qualifications, even
though he hoped he would never have to work outside football.
He had collected eight GCE 'O' levels and then one 'A' level
in Russian; he was taking more 'A' levels in French and
English at night school and intending to take an external BA
degree in Russian.

There was an impressive, cool resolution about him: three
nights of studying a week, no dancing, strict application to
training, a definite statement that he would be married in
February 1969. He and the younger of his two footballer
brothers lived in the same digs in Sheffield and went home every
weekend. His father was partially reconciled to the situation.
'The boss has been to see him, and my father thinks he is a
great gentleman,' said Kazimierz, the tiniest of satisfied smiles
flickering in his face.

Kazimierz summed up the story by saying: 'We were just sure we were going to be footballers – especially Bezek; he was mad keen.' He said his youngest brother, 11-year-old Tadeusz, would definitely be a professional player as well.

4 Tragedy

In the 1951–2 season Sheffield Wednesday scored 100 goals to win promotion back into Division One of the Football League. Forty-six of the goals were scored by their memorably resourceful, ginger-haired centre-forward, Derek Dooley, who was 22 and weighed over $13\frac{1}{2}$ stone. Less than a year after that marvellous performance Dooley, injured in a characteristic collision with a goalkeeper, had to have his right leg amputated from the middle of the thigh.

The tragedies in football are specially affecting because of the youth and public adoration of the victims. Dooley was a local favourite, born in the working-class Sheffield of outside lavatories in communal yards and low wages for tough work, and he was playing for the team he admired devotedly as a boy. He was Thunderboots, propelled from obscurity in grimed streets to national fame by his ability to force his way past other big men in a penalty area and lash a football past a goalkeeper. He was a Saturday hero by, of, and for the people, his identity contained and gladly expressed in his football.

Dooley, smoking his pipe in 1967, described the accident which ended his playing career fourteen years before in clear detail. It happened in a match against Preston North End at Preston in February 1953, which had its own irony since the first League game Dooley ever played was on the same ground. He said: 'Preston played the offside game very effectively. So

to beat it we had this move worked out. Whoever got the ball
had to release it very quickly, before the Preston defence could
move up. Well, Albert Quixall released the ball from well back,
and I chased it. George Thompson, the Preston goalkeeper,
hesitated and then came out. Now I'd run from the half-way
line – you know, a big bloke, 13 stone 10 lb. I connected with
the ball just as George stuck his leg out and caught me just
above the ankle. That was it.'

Dooley blamed no one for his injury. He said: 'I'd been in
worse mix-ups – far worse scrimmages than that. It was a
straightforward incident.' Then he said: 'I put the ball past
him. It's my one regret in all this that the ball didn't finish in
the net.' Nobody could ask more of a hero than that flat, rueful
afterthought.

The environment which produced Dooley was the one which
had nurtured professional football itself. He was born in 1929
in Pitsmoor, in the west end of Sheffield, where the city meanders
in a smoky, greasy straggle of workshops into Rotherham. It
was, as Dooley descriptively put it, 'the works end'. He is a
frank, even ebullient talker now, made fluent by a great deal
of addressing sportsmen's dinners, churchmen's groups and
hospital patients, but there is an endearing simplicity in his
delivery. He refers to himself a lot as 'Derek' and links his
material with amused, public speaker's phrases such as, 'Let
me hasten to add' and 'I don't mind telling you'. This is the
authentic plain man pushed by circumstances into story-telling,
and doing his duty diligently by it.

His father was a steel worker, who had his share of unem-
ployment in the thirties, but Dooley remembers his parents
as generous whenever they could be. They bought him his
first pair of football boots when he was 11, when he went to
Oller Lane Intermediate School, where 'you could take the

School Certificate if you were one of the brighter ones' but also where 'football was on the curriculum – two periods a week'.

His home, in Bramber Street, Pitsmoor, was one of four houses in the same yard, and it was there that most of his football was first learned. 'Times many,' he said, 'I've put the ball through a window, or broken one with me shoe coming off.' The penalties were not severe. His father understood that compulsion for football; he had once had a trial game with Bradford City. It was not, of course, a real football that went through the windows. That sort of luxurious possession was out of reach. Usually it was one of those black, fairly solid rubber balls which would also be used for summer cricket in the same yard.

Dooley and his friends used to organize makeshift matches, in which one street would play another, on the gloomy recreation grounds in the area: patches of grit and oily grass, hemmed in by the crouched streets, with the rusty swings and roundabouts which creaked under a cafuffle of ragged children. Jackets made goal posts, and: 'If you went down you got up with a lump of cinder in your knee.'

His secondary school had classes composed of twenty boys and twenty girls. Dooley was made captain of his class, because: 'You know how it was at school – if you could fight you were in charge.' He picked the football team by naming all his closest friends, 'and then a few of the lads who could play a bit'. He picked himself at centre-forward. 'Of course I did,' he said. 'For the simple reason that you always wanted to be the bloke putting the ball in the back of the net. If you couldn't be that you wanted to be goalkeeper.'

Oller Lane took its football solemnly, even if it had no sports field of its own. The school team played its matches on Firth

Park Grammar School's pitch, and the one match Dooley's school liked to win more than any other was the one against the grammar school. 'We wanted to beat them because we knew they were better,' he said. 'They had better facilities, better everything. Throughout my life it's always been important to me to win.'

Now that Dooley has seen a great deal of modern schools' football, as a celebrity, he is knowledgeable about the differences between working-class childhood of the thirties and forties and that of the sixties. He won his school colours at 13, playing in a team of average age between 15 and 16. He said that after the age of 10 he was 'always above average height, and never skinny with it'. He said: 'When someone threw a shirt at you and said, "That's yours now till you leave school", well, that was something. To be allowed to take it home and ask your mother to wash it was something out of this world. Probably nowadays if you did that to a lad he'd throw it back at you and say, "Let me have it back when it's clean."'

He sees schoolboys' football as far better organized, better coached, better equipped than he knew it. 'It applies right from the start, right from a thing like transport. Nowadays they go off to a match in a group. In our day if Fred missed his tram, there wasn't another for half an hour and that was that. Someone else played or they went on a man short till he turned up. And look at the coaching. There are far more two-footed players about now. The chap who used to take us – our games master was the geography master who had one arm – he used to shout and bawl at us a bit, but that was all. If we couldn't kick with our left foot that was all there was to it.' But he could not imagine any boy enjoying football more than he did, whatever the encouragement.

Dooley got into senior football, as many other professionals from South Yorkshire have, through the opportunities given him by the Sheffield YMCA. He joined because it offered the kind of facilities that schools have now. Its guiding hand was an avuncular but authoritarian figure known as Pop Bennett, or, as Dooley alternatively called him, Mester Bennett. 'I joined for football,' he said. 'They had their own playing field. I saw Mester Bennett, and he said, "Where do you play?" I said, "Centre-forward." He said, "We've got one." This was for the under-16 side. He said, "You're a big lad, we'll put you at centre-half." Well, we lost 6–5 the first time I played, but I scored four goals from the centre-half position. But I hasten to add that their centre-forward scored five of theirs.'

After this game Pop Bennett complained to Dooley: 'Well, you're no centre-half, are you?' Dooley remembered: 'I said to him, "I told you that." So he said, "We'll have you at left back for the next game." I scored two that time. After that he played me at centre-forward. I got into the Sheffield District under-16 side.'

He was still 15 when he got home from work (in a hearing-aid factory) one Friday evening to find a telegram which said, as nearly as he could remember it twenty-three years later: 'Selected to play Lincoln City Reserves against Denaby United. Report Tickhill Square Denaby.' He recalled that Mester Bennett was not at all pleased when he told him he would not be playing for the YMCA the following day. The call, mysterious and dramatic, was irresistible. He said: 'I've never known how I got involved with Lincoln City. I suppose someone must have been watching me.'

One has to remember the static nature of working-class life in the forties to understand Dooley's excitement at the journey, let alone the beckoning from a professional football club. He said: 'Before this I'd never been out of Sheffield, except for the annual holiday that was invariably taken at Blackpool. Black-pool without fail. Denaby was like the end of the earth. I had to set off at half past ten in the morning to get a bus, and then after that I had to get a tram. We lost 6–1 and I scored our goal.'

There was one distressing moment for the boy to mar this pleasurable event. 'When I got there someone threw me a red and white shirt to play in. Well, I didn't know what Lincoln's colours were. But that was sacrilege to me because Sheffield United played in red and white. I was a Wednesday-ite. In Sheffield you had to be one or the other.' This was not feigned hurt. For Dooley at 15, just as applies even now to some totally committed club fans, the guilty sense of treachery in such a situation was real.

Dooley played for Lincoln, in the old Third Division (North), for two years, appearing mostly in the reserves but occasionally in the League team. The reserves side played in the Midland League, and he remembered the experience as invaluable in toughening him for first-class football. 'There was a fair bit of shoe dished out,' he said. 'They had a lot of old League players who were finishing their careers, and they knew all the tricks of the trade. They were playing for about £5 a time, and it really mattered to them. It taught me how to take care of myself. I had to take a fair bit of boot. I was much younger, you see. They were trying to intimidate me.'

He thought the professionals' bonus for winning a match in the Midland League then was ten shillings. He was an amateur, being paid between £1 and £1 10s for expenses. 'But you've got to remember,' he said, 'that in those days I could go down into Lincoln and have a meal and get back to Sheffield, and I'd got change. I suppose I used to come out of it five shillings a week to the good.'

Dooley accepted the harsh treatment he got as a young player as being very much a proper part of the game. 'I was a fair size, of course. When I was 16 I was touching 6 foot. I got a few cuts and bruises, but I've got no regrets. It's a man's game, after all.'

No sport could have been more competitive. He said: 'Nobody was ever averse to catching you on one leg and having you over, or coming up behind and giving you a good dig. I suppose I was a bit rough and crude myself at the time – no great shakes as a footballer. I probably went in where angels would fear to tread, as they say. I don't think it was courage. It was just youth. A bit later on I learned to say, "Right, I'm not going in among that little lot." I don't think any of these players had any intention of having me carried off on a stretcher. I was a young lad, and they wanted to steady me down a bit.'

But clearly only the toughest could survive such an environment. The pressure was not confined only to physical aggression. He remembered: 'Some of these blokes would say, "Right, Dooley, you'll get no bloody goals today, lad, or I'll break both your legs." They had no real intention of trying to do it, but they'd come in really strong. I knew when I went out on to the field, and I'd scored two or three goals the week before, any bloke that had any salt about him at all was bound to have a go at me.'

Dooley, vigorous, upright, powerful-looking still, in spite of his stiff artificial limb under the thick, tweed trouser leg, epitomizes the footballer of the forties and fifties. It is difficult to picture this honest, industrial yeoman in the clever-headed, lissom setting of the football of this decade. There are big men in the game today, of course, and players as ruthless as the ones he grew up with; but the tone is different, his attitude to aggressiveness both more familiar and yet less knowing. He sees much petulance in the modern players' less studied, more eruptive violence.

He said: 'I've seen more players sent off or had their names taken in the last two or three seasons than happened in all the years I was playing. I think players should accept a bit of boot. Nowadays a bloke gets knocked and he turns round and he's got someone round the throat. In the old days he'd just say, "Right, I'll get him next time round."'

He acknowledges the problems confronting present-day forwards by the more ordered, more perceptive defences; but he is irritated by forwards who lose their tempers in the frustration that comes from being marked out of a game. He remembered a match against Brentford, when he was playing for Sheffield Wednesday, in which he scored all three goals in a 3–2 win, Brentford's centre-half being Ron Greenwood, now West Ham's manager. He said: 'I found I could beat Ron for speed, although I know when it came to playing football he had me skint. Anyway, when it comes to the return match I find that not only have I got Ronnie on one side of me, right up close, but there's the right-half, who's about 6 foot 2 inches, on the other, and he's crowding me as well. All right, here we are at half-time, we're winning 3–0 and I haven't scored. Well, that's all right. I'm not running round pulling someone's shirt. If they're marking me that tight I'm taking them out of the game. You've got to be big enough and man enough to stand this. This is what it's all about.' His meticulous memory of the detail of his career prompted another footnote: 'We won that game 5–2 in the end. I scored one in a scrimmage.'

When Dooley joined Sheffield Wednesday at 17½ he was far from an immediate success. The week after his first game in the League side he played for the reserves, and the week after that he was in the 'A' team. It took him a year to get back into the first team, and then he was immediately dropped. It makes the tragedy of his exit from the game all the more poignant that his fame was established in a single, dazzling League season. Being a big, brave and entirely frank man, he does not appreciate, I think, how affecting are some of the things he says. He was talking casually, fondly, about the business of being a footballer, and he said: 'It's a funny thing, this football career. It's something you don't really expect to get. As a boy you dream about it. You imagine it a lot. But it's hard to accept you'll ever make it. You don't really ever believe you're going to run on the field for the first team.'

The dream came true. Thunderboots had his name in headlines, and children bounced round him in the street. In October 1951, Sheffield Wednesday were well down in the Second Division table, and they had tried six different centre-forwards. Dooley was given another chance in the reserves team against Bolton Wanderers, and in front of half of the Wednesday board of directors scored four goals. The following week he played for the League side against Burnley and scored two goals from the edge of the penalty box in a 2–1 win. Wednesday's 100-goal season was under way; Dooley was rushing courageously, devastatingly towards public adulation and personal disaster.

Again comes the innocent poignancy in Dooley's story. 'In those days at 22 you were still a young kid in a football team. Most of the side then could give me about eight years or more. I never really settled in the team until I'd had about twelve matches.'

The collision with the Preston goalkeeper broke his leg, and he was taken to hospital. He remembers hearing a whispered conversation among doctors near his bed. He had gangrene. A few hours later all that was left of his right leg was a six-inch stump.

C

Dooley recalled his situation plainly: 'I was 23, I'd been married the June before. I'd no house, no trade. I was living with my parents. I'd banked a bit of money, but it wasn't much. The maximum wage was £14, and the bonus for a win was £2 10s. I got £42 for winning the Second Division championship. I think if someone had said it to me in so many words that I'd never play football again I'd have said, "Well, life's not worth living." But no one ever put it just like that, and after a bit, lying there, I got a bit stronger, and I said, "Well, Derek, except for the fact that you can't play football you can live a normal life."'

His club held a benefit match and opened a subscription fund for him; the local evening newspaper opened a public fund which produced £2,000, enough to buy him a house. A man, who never allowed Dooley to know his name, sent him £3,000 out of £100,000 he had won on the football pools. Letters from fans poured in by the thousand.

He said: 'Until then I hadn't realized how much people had taken to me. When I started getting about people would stop me in the street and say, "Lad, you've given me hours of enjoyment." They were sincere. I got letters by the sackful when I got home.'

He was offered the licence of a pub, but eventually took a job as telephonist at a bakery, and he stayed there for eight years, leaving the firm when he was its assistant sales manager. He went back to Sheffield Wednesday in 1962 to take charge of the club's development fund, a fulltime job which keeps him in close contact with the supporters and the players. The return, he admitted, 'twanged at the heart strings a bit'. He watches a lot of football and talks about it eagerly: a dyed-in-the-wool Sheffield Wednesday supporter.

Outside the ground small boys, who were not born at the

time he was knocked abruptly and cruelly out of football, gather round him with their picture books of players with Beatle haircuts. 'Sign this, Mester Dooley,' they shout. 'Please, Derek.'

Anyone who was in Manchester in February 1958, particularly if he lived there, as I did, will remember for ever the stunning impact on the city of the air crash at Munich airport which killed eight of Manchester United's players. The shock was followed, just as it is in particularly closely tied families after a death, by a lingering communal desolation. No other tragedy in sport has been as brutal or as affecting as this one.

It was not simply that very popular athletes had been killed and a brilliantly promising team destroyed. There was a general youthfulness about this particular Manchester United team which was new to the game. Manchester relished this fact. The old, often gloomy city had a shining exuberance to acclaim. These young players were going to take the country, and probably Europe too, by storm. To identify with this precociousness, to watch people in other towns marvelling and conceding defeat, gave a surge to the spirit. Suddenly most of the team was dead.

The players killed were Roger Byrne, Geoff Bent, Eddie Colman, Duncan Edwards, David Pegg, Mark Jones, Tommy Taylor, Bill Whelan. Four of them were England international players, Byrne and Edwards and Taylor all being firmly established with appearances in the England side well into double figures. Pegg had been capped once. It was the death of Duncan Edwards which gave the deepest, most lasting pain to the community. This was not because he was liked personally any more than the others, but because there was a special appeal to people's ideals about him. Walter Winterbottom, the England team manager at the time, called him 'the spirit of British football'. He meant the football that exists in children's daydreams and good men's hopes: honest, brilliant and irresistibly strong.

There was extra poignancy in Edwards's death in that he lived for fifteen days after the crash. How bitterly that hurt. One of the key components in Duncan Edwards's appeal was his size. Big men in sport are always specially compelling, whether they lumber comically or endear by their dogged willingness. Edwards at 21 was a six-footer, weighing $13\frac{1}{2}$ stone, but with the immense presence he brought to his game he had nimbleness as well as strength, flair as well as calm.

A youth so equipped was bound to prompt affectionate epithets from sportswriters and fans, and people cudgelled their brains to find new ones. He was Kid Dynamite, the Baby Giant, the Gentle Giant, Big Dunk, the Boy with the Heart of a Man. As the daily reports came in from the hospital in Munich, Manchester raised hope for his survival. In the second week after the crash people began to talk in their ready, sentimental clichés about the Lionheart fighting his way through again. There was much banality in the words, but the longing was sincere. Then he died.

Edwards was born in October 1936, in Dudley, Worcestershire. As a schoolboy of the forties and a teenager of the fifties he was part of the generation which linked the hard, sombre days of the war and rationing with the more dashing, mobile times which followed in such animated reaction. He would be in his early 30s now and, if still playing football, which is likely, assuredly an old-fashioned-looking figure among the imitating contemporaries of George Best. He had dignity on the field always, even in his teens: that senior officer kind of authority which comes to few players and then late in career, as with Danny Blanchflower, Jimmy Armfield, George Cohen.

I looked through an album of photographs in Edwards's parents' home, which showed him right through his life. The face was grave, the gaze he gave at the world open and tranquil. Winterbottom's description was not fanciful, in spite of being one which any thoughtful man would hesitate to use in connection with any player. Edwards represented the kind of self-respecting modesty which is not nurtured in the ferocity of the modern game. It has not been deliberately forced out of football; it is just not natural to the age.

The album had pictures of Edwards in his street clothes, as well as in football strips, and in them the period was caught, fixed by his personality. He was bulky in those ill-fitting jackets and wide trousers with broad turn-ups. Clothes did not interest young footballers then; there was neither enough money nor a teenage-identity industry to exploit such an interest. He could have been a young miner freshly scrubbed for a night at the Labour Club dance. He did not look important, in the celebrated sense; he looked as if he mattered, and belonged, to his family and his friends. The anonymity of style was true to his generation and his kind.

The situation was very different when he put his football boots on. I went to see Mr Geoff Groves, the headmaster of a secondary school in Dudley, who was one of Edwards's teachers when the boy was at primary school. Mr Groves remembered this 11-year-old playing for the school team against a neighbouring school the day after Edwards had got home from a spell of hop-picking. He said: 'He dominated the whole match. He told all the other twenty-one players what to do, and the referee and both the linesmen. When I got home that evening I wrote to a friend and said I'd just seen a boy of 11 who would play for England one day.'

A year later, Mr Groves said, the boy was playing 'in the

style of a man, with wonderful balance and colossal power in
his shot'. Already he was showing the intelligence in his game
which became central to all he did. 'He already understood
all about distribution of the ball,' said Mr Groves. 'And he was
such a dominating player that the ball seemed to come to him
wherever he was.' It is one of the distinguishing marks of the
most talented players that they always seem to have the ball
exactly when they want it.

Edwards was a heroic figure in Dudley long before he became
a professional player. He became captain of the English schoolboys' side, having joined it when he was 13, and many of the
leading clubs were clamouring for his signature. Matt Busby
called at his home at 2 a.m. on the morning after his 16th
birthday and acquired him for United. He was 16½ when he
played his first match for United, 6 feet tall and weighing
12 stone 6 lb. At 18½ he became the youngest player ever to be
picked for the full England international team. It was the one
which beat Scotland 7-2 at Wembley in April 1955, and this
was the company he was in:

Williams (Wolves); Meadows (Manchester City), Byrne
(Manchester United); Phillips (Portsmouth), Wright (Wolves,
captain), Edwards; Matthews (Blackpool), Revie (Manchester
City), Lofthouse (Bolton Wanderers), Wilshaw (Wolves),
Blunstone (Chelsea).

Sir Stanley Matthews, who was 40 when he played in that
match, told me that he thought Edwards could truly be called
unique. To Matthews, who learned his football in the days
when, as he put it, 'they all said you had to be strong, with
big, thick thighs', Edwards's build was no surprise. 'But,' he
said, 'he was so quick, and that was what made the difference.
I can't remember any other player that size who was quick
like that.'

The point was emphasized eighteen months later, when Edwards, normally a left-half, was placed at inside-left in the England team against Denmark, when the forward line was: Matthews, Brooks (Tottenham Hotspur), Taylor, Edwards, Finney (Preston North End). Edwards scored twice and Taylor three times in England's win, which gives an indication of the scoring power Manchester United had at their command.

The fondness Manchester United's supporters felt for this player was expressed in the common adulation by boys but also in the quiet admiration of the kind which fathers show for successful sons when they speak about them to neighbours, and out of the boys' hearing. In this regard for Edwards there was often a sad sympathy for opposing players who were being crushed coldly out of the game by him. I remember watching one of United's home matches when beside me was a supporter in his 50s, who shouted little but nodded his head nearly all the time in deep satisfaction, letting out occasionally an equally deep sigh which was eloquent in its pleasure. By the middle of the first half one of the opposition's inside-forwards – I forget, I am ashamed to say, the team involved, but perhaps this is also kindness – was reacting furiously to the frustration of being treated like a small child by Edwards, firmly but without viciousness or even very much concern. The player threw himself several times at Edwards, either missing the moving body entirely or bouncing off it, and on each occasion the man beside me sucked in his breath, shook his head and said softly: 'Nay, lad, not with 'im, not with 'im.' It was the decent, absorbed football fan like this one for whom Winterbottom was speaking when he called Edwards the spirit of British football.

Edwards's funeral took place at St Francis's Church, Dudley, not far from his home. There were at least 5,000 people outside the church. The vicar made it a footballer's service. He said:

'He goes to join the memorable company of Steve Bloomer and Alex James.' Had he lived long enough Edwards would surely have joined the company of England team captains. Instead he left a memory of brilliance and courage and a sense of vast promise he was not allowed to fulfil.

His grave in Dudley cemetery is elaborate. The headstone has an ingrained picture of him in football kit holding a ball above his head for a throw-in. An inscription reads: 'A Day of Memory, sad to recall. Without Farewell, He Left Us All.' There are three flower stands, and one of them is in the shape of a football. It suits the nature of his class and his neighbourhood, and it is attended with great care by his father, a gardener at the cemetery.

His father, Mr Gladstone Edwards, felt he had to explain why he was working at the cemetery. He said: 'People think I came to this job because he's here. But that wasn't the reason. I had to change my work, and I've always liked flowers and gardening. I felt I wanted to be out of doors.' Duncan was his only child.

Neither he nor his wife could hide the depth of their loss. Nor was there any reason why they should try. When I went to see them Duncan Edwards had been dead for nine years, and Mr Edwards, at least, could talk about his son straightforwardly, although all the time with a quiet deliberation. He said that even then there was still a steady trickle of visitors to Duncan's grave. There were days when twenty people would arrive to look at it, like pilgrims. They seldom knew that the gardener they stopped to talk to was the player's father. They nearly always said the same thing: that there would never be another Duncan. Mr Edwards added that Friday often brought the most visitors, and they were often lorry-drivers with Manchester accents. They had stopped on their long run home from somewhere south. The next day, of course, they would be at Old Trafford to watch the match.

In Mr and Mrs Edwards's small, semi-detached house the front room is kept shaded and spotless. It was in here that Mr Edwards showed me Duncan's photograph album, and also let me open a glass-fronted display cabinet and examine the mementoes of Duncan's life. It contained eighteen of his caps at full international, youth and schoolboy level, to represent the eighteen times that he played in his country's senior team. Each was kept brushed and was filled inside with tissue paper. On top of the cabinet were three framed photographs of Duncan: one taken in uniform when he was in the Army, doing his National Service, another with his fiancée and a third in which he wears a Manchester United shirt. Beside them was a framed £5 note, which was the last present he gave his mother. The tiny room was dominated by a portrait of Edwards in his England shirt, the frame 2 feet wide by 2½ long. The room was a shrine.

That showcase also had a copy of the order of service which was used on the day that two stained-glass windows were dedicated to Edwards at St Francis's Church. They are close to the font, beside a picture of a gentle Jesus which was given to the church by a mother, in memory of a baby girl. One of the windows has Edwards down on one knee, and there is a scroll running across his chest which says: 'God is with us for our Captain.' All the survivors of the Munich crash were in the church when the windows were dedicated by the Bishop of Worcester in August 1961. Busby said at the service: 'These windows should keep the name of Duncan Edwards alive for ever, and shine as a monument and example to the youth of Dudley and England.'

Edwards's name is also kept in front of the people of Dudley in the title of the Duncan Edwards Social Club, which is attached to the town football club, and in two trophies for local schools football.

These memorials commemorate not only Duncan Edwards's football but also the simple decency of the man. He represented thousands in their wish for courage, acclaim and rare talent, and he had all three without swagger. The hero is the creature other people would like to be. Edwards was such a man, and he enabled people to respect themselves more.

In January 1965 three of England's best known footballers were sent to prison for four months after their conviction in what was called The Soccer Conspiracy Case. They were Peter Swan, the Sheffield Wednesday centre-half who had played nineteen times for his country, David Layne, the Sheffield Wednesday centre-forward, and Tony Kay, a wing-half, formerly of Sheffield Wednesday but at the time of the disclosure playing for Everton. The gist of the case was that all three, while playing for Wednesday, had conspired to prevent their own team from winning a match to facilitate a betting coup. A few months after the case the three players were suspended from football for life by the Football Association, which meant that any form of officially recognized football anywhere was barred to them. Kay and Swan had pleaded not guilty in court.

The case made a wretched winter for British football. Seven less well-known players and former players were sentenced at the same time on similar charges to terms of imprisonment ranging from four years to six months. The exposure was the work of *The People*, the Sunday newspaper, whose reporters did their job resourcefully and ruthlessly, and the dirty shrapnel of the explosion nicked and wounded people all round the game. Such a revelation was bound to make the public ask each other, blackly, how much 'fixing' of matches was going on which was never discovered. This fear struck at the very roots and heart of football. The footballers, once found guilty, were bound to suffer the complete punishment.

While the tale was being told little sympathy was invited for the men concerned, although Mr. Justice Lawton, passing sentence, said he accepted that the Sheffield Wednesday players were involved 'really by chance' and on one isolated occasion; they presented him, he said, 'with the most unpleasant part of my duty'. Excuse may never be possible, but at least the personal tragedy of the event should be acknowledged. The fallen, ruined hero is no figure for callous scorn. Some respected men in the game have given their names to appeals for the players' reinstatement. There is kindness here but also, I think, a failure on their part to recognize the significance of the case. Perhaps it is a matter of being too close to the game to see the extent of the damage. A court conviction on a charge of 'fixing' football is not just a nasty blotch on the wall, but a jagged hole in the fabric. Two or three more like that and the whole structure falls in rubble.

Of the three men I have named, Kay was the most colourful player, and he was notably articulate. He was 27 at the time of the case, and he had played once for England, against Switzerland. He was an extremely tough, quick, enterprising halfback, of the combative, all-action kind: very much the type of player whom Sir Alf Ramsey developed in Nobby Stiles for England's World Cup victory. Stiles played magnificently for England. It is fair to ask whether he would have been given the chance if Kay had been available. That thought was very sharply in my mind when I went to see Kay in Liverpool in 1967.

He looked haggard, although not in the debilitated sense of a man gone to seed. He looked what he was still: a hard-driven athlete, the flesh tight on the bones. He had red, scrubbing-brush hair, and he wore thick-rimmed glasses. He exuded an exaggerated ruefulness, a bitter and aggressive self-mockery. There was a distinct television-age, showbiz edge to the back-street wit. 'The cops have it in for me; must have,' he said. 'Have you ever heard of anyone being booked for parking by a copper on a horse? That's Anthony's luck.'

Kay was brought up in Sheffield, and he learned about life and football, which amounted practically to the same thing for him, in the same atmosphere which Derek Dooley had des-cribed. His experience even had some of the identical physical characteristics, but encountered ten years later: the street football, the Sheffield YMCA, even Pop Bennett. He knew working-class austerity as people know sweat, through the pores, not book-learnt or observed in passing. Money was important because there was not much of it about. Everton bought him from Sheffield Wednesday for more than £55,000.

The face has a flare of insolence, and now that he had much to regret he played up this component in his personality, telling stories of the persecution and recurrent disaster in his life with a chirpy, gritty comicality. 'Wasn't I always in trouble?' he said. 'Well, I nearly got killed more than once, didn't I? Look how the crowds used to get at me.'

He launched into a story about a match in London, which ended with a mob of the home crowd's fans yelling for his blood round the exit. He walked out disguised in the home team manager's long overcoat and trilby. He said: 'When I got in the coach I took 'em off and tapped the window at the crowd. You should have seen 'em,' and he bared his teeth wide and crooked his fingers on either side of his face, like talons.

Then he said: 'There was that time in Italy when the crowd was at me. "Kay, Bastardo, Bastardo." They were behind this wire grille (bared teeth and crooked fingers again). I banged the ball at their faces. So what happens when we come off at the end? I'm there, with our team in the dressing-room, and I'm standing at the tunnel thanking everyone, and I go up to this Italian trainer, who's only about 7 feet tall. I hold my hand out, and what does he do? He's only got both me arms pinned behind me back. And all the Italian team's giving me one as they go off the field.'

The resentment poured out of him, as he built up a picture of a victimized upbringing. The voice teetered up into a thin malevolence, the voice of childhood's tormentors: 'Right, you've been very, very naughty, and now we're going to rattle your little arse. Whack. Sort that out.'

Kay, the bolshie; Kay, the whipping-boy; Kay, the misunderstood; Kay, the unlucky: he overstated his battering from life, and his fumbling resistance, with the skill of a natural comedian who is beginning to believe the letter as well as the spirit of his material.

'I've always hated referees,' he said. 'To me they're all no-marks. Otherwise, they wouldn't be there. Who are they? All the week they're sitting there in offices, scribbling away, scribble, scribble, and on Saturday afternoons they're on the field with all the big men, and they're saying, "Right, now you do what I tell you or you're going in my little book."' He did a wickedly observed impersonation of a hunchbacked, myopic referee writing in a notebook, his hands up by his nose. He said: 'I've seen blokes kicking lumps out of each other, and what's the referee doing? He's wagging his finger and making a great production out of moving the ball three foot back for a free kick.'

Kay's sadly funny performance was the more disturbing because in his comment on authority, and its view of him,

there was a strong thread of truth. As a player he was undoubtedly one of those eruptive influences which infuriate
referees. He was known for his bitter tackling and only tough
men were prepared to take the consequences. Kay insisted to
me that he was a marked man not only in the opposition's
dressing-room but in the referee's as well, and he aded that he
did not mind telling referees so. One of his troubles was that he
was never discreet in what he said or what he did. He said to me:
'I was naïve.' He was right. He knew most of the tricks of the
trade, but not the most important trick of all, which is to appear
not to.

The more Kay talks the stronger is the conviction borne in
on the listener that his misfortunes were impelled from inside
him. Like everyone else the influences he assimilated from his
environment were an imperfect blend; but is it the mixture or
the chemistry which makes a man? Kay was embattled against
the world, pretty well all of it, so that ultimately he was working
against himself. Even in trivial, everyday matters, such as his
relationship with road traffic, his progress was interrupted by
violent incidents of bizarre complexity, in which his saving
grace was to be found in his comic, fatalistic hindsight. One
accident, as he described it, involved the inexorable will of
some dauntless old lady, launched come what might for the
distant haven of the opposite pavement. There was also snow
and a steep hill. Then: 'So all of a sudden I'm waking up in
me mini, upside down, and this geezer's shouting all sorts at
me out of his bedroom winder.' On another occasion the slap-
stick disaster ends: 'So here I am, can't move a limb, being
wheeled about the station by a porter on a trolley.'

Kay managed to squeeze a few wicked, retaliatory jokes out
of his prison sentence. He said that the prison governor was 'a
wild football fan, and he couldn't get enough of the game'. Kay

said that he and his friends were given full rein to train the prison football team, and that the governor refereed most of the matches himself. 'We only lost one game out of fourteen,' Kay said, adding with a look of feigned distaste, 'and that was because the other lot brought their own referee; the game was *bent*.' He laughed. He said that the first warder he met in gaol was a little man – most villains in Kay's life are little men – who greeted him with: 'Yes, it's through people like you I never win the pools.' Kay said: 'I thought to myself, "Hullo, Anthony, you've found yourself one here. It's your luck again."' He encountered the warder later when the man was a linesman at one of the matches. The story is a symmetry of irony:

'The governor was sold on us. I gave 'em all hell, you know. He used to say, "Well done, young Kay." Well, this little warder – the bad one – he kept sticking his flag up and shouting at me every time I touched anybody. After a bit I said to him, "Why don't you piss off?" He was furious. He said, "I'll have you yet." So I ran across to the governor – he was refereeing again – and I said, "Excuse me, Sir, can't you do something about this linesman? He keeps on at me. I can't concentrate." So the governor went across to this warder, and he said, "Not so much noise, please, Mr So-and-so."' Kay's eyes glinted at the memory.

To judge from Kay's conversation, his attitude to authority always had that cynicism. He reminds one of the bad lad at the back of the class, or the hard case in the barrack-room, who recognizes the sneaking respect, and often fear, that the man in charge has for the ones who won't conform. Such men seldom appeal for help, and when they do it is to exploit the boss's sense of importance. Kay told me this story about a match against Fulham:

'I was up against Jimmy Hill, and he was up there towering

above me. Every time I went up for the ball there he was, just leaning over the top of me. I thought, "Right, I'm not having this all the game. Next time we go up I'll have his shorts off him." Well, up we went, and I shoved me hand out and I missed 'em. Instead I caught him right between the legs. He screamed the place down. But he kept with me afterwards, all over the field. I went to the ref. I said, "Hey, ref, look at this maniac with the beard. Look at the way he's after me." It worked.' Kay's relished little triumphs can only be properly understood by someone brought up where people never play cards for matchsticks.

. . I was warned before I went to see him that Kay might be sad; that if the gloom was on him he might even weep. He anticipated my wariness. He had stopped crying, he said, although when he was first told that he could never play football competitively again, he confessed: 'I never cried so much in all me life.' He said it looking straight at me, using the words like a showbiz catchphrase, but not smiling. He knew he had been overdoing the clowning. 'It just hides the tears,' he said. 'You can't cry all the time. You get a reputation for it. No one wants to know after a bit. They say, "Oh Christ, I've got to put up with this crying gett again." You can't just give up, can you?'

It was plain that he had been deeply hurt by what had happened to him; he was convinced it had been imposed and not brought upon him by himself. Every six months, he said, he wrote to the FA, asking if they would reconsider his registration. He did not really think they ever would. People in Liverpool, he said, were friendly and sympathetic towards him. That salty city would never snub a man like Kay. He was as much one of Liverpool's own, pugnacious and at least pretending cunning, as if he had been born there.

But his life was not pleasing him, to say the least of it. At the time I was talking to him he was a family man living away from his wife, and a bookmaker not sure that there would be another year's wages out of his betting shop. What had he been doing since prison? 'Just going round in circles,' he said. 'Getting nowhere.'

He had been playing football, surreptitiously, in scratch matches, giving another name when he was asked, keeping an eye open for men hanging about with cameras. He was training twice a week, and I could believe it when he said: 'I really push myself.' He did much of his training at a school gymnasium, often giving practical instruction to the boys. He said, the edge going out of the voice for the first time: 'They all want to take me on, you know. They think, "Oh, this old Tony Kay, he's finished." I like to get 'em trying to get past me on the outside, and I'm leaving 'em behind, and I'm shouting, "Come on, what are you waiting for, you lads?"'

There was a lot of heart in Kay as a player. Professional sport made him, tested him and broke him. He is one of football's tragic casualties because he was so strongly equipped in nearly all his aspects. His counsel said in court, after his conviction: 'He has given up for £100 what has in fact been one of the greatest careers of any footballer. He was tempted once, and fell.'

5 Eulogy

Everyone who follows football has his favourite player; even the players do. The selection is bound to reflect something of the nature of the one who is doing the choosing. The favourite is not necessarily being named as the greatest player of all. We may admit, reluctantly, our favourite's weaknesses. What we are saying is that this particular player appeals to us more than any other. It has to do with his personality, his style of behaviour, perhaps importantly the way in which he compensates for his deficiencies. He is the player who may disappoint sometimes with a ragged, off-form performance, and yet over the years stays clear and bright in the memory. He is the player we bring to mind first when we ask ourselves what football looks like when we enjoy it most. The man I name for this role is Bobby Charlton.

The flowing line of Charlton's football has no disfiguring barbs in it, but there is a heavy and razor-sharp arrowhead at its end. It is the combination of the graceful and the dramatic which makes him so special. There are few players who affect a crowd's responses as much as he does. Something extraordinary is expected of him the moment he receives the ball. He can silence a crowd instantly, make it hold its breath in expectation. A shot from Charlton, especially if hit on the run from outside the penalty area, is one of the great events of the sport, not because it is rare, which it is not, but because the power of it is massive and it erupts out of elegance; he is never clumsy or desperate in movement; he can rise very close to the athletic ideal.

The persistent complaint I have heard made against Charlton, the one which keeps him out of the lists when some people name the handful of the world's greatest players, is that he avoids the fury of the game, that where the hacking and elbowing are fiercest Charlton is not to be found. But this is like dismissing Dickens from the world's great literature because he never went to gaol for throwing bricks at politicians; like denigrating Disraeli on the grounds that he was a third-rate novelist. Charlton's courage is geared to his special talents. I have certainly never seen him fling himself headlong across his own goalmouth to head the ball away from some opposing forward's foot. But I have seen him summon his speed and use his swerve to score goals when defences were swinging their boots at him with intent to hurt. Charlton has been felled so often in his career that he could not possibly have stayed so compellingly in the game for so long if he lacked nerve. I do not object at all that he has never been sent off the field for kneeing someone in the groin.

It is true, I think, to say that although he became an England international player when he was 20 it was in later years that he gathered full resolution for the game. He was never less than an excellent player, but he was past 25 before he became a great one. He flowered fully, and gloriously, for the World Cup in 1966, appropriately scoring England's first goal with a veering run from near the centre-circle and a characteristic shot taken in mid-stride. He scored another like it in the semi-final against Portugal. They are the kind of goals he will be remembered by. They are a great player's goals.

Yet Charlton is not just a scoring specialist. Being so fast and possessing the best body swerve of his generation, he made his name as a winger. In his early years as a professional his great merit was his ability to run past the defender from the left touchline and go diagonally on the back's inside to hit the ball at goal with either foot. This was the young Charlton, with most of his weight in his legs, whose speed and control of the ball were aimed almost exclusively at scoring goals. By his late 20s – he was 28 in the 1966 World Cup – he had moved to a deep-lying centre-forward or inside-forward position, as the fulcrum of the attack. His accuracy with the ball at great distance was now used to shift, in one sudden pass, the point of action. These passes, especially if preceded by one of his sidesteps and a burst of acceleration, could turn the fortune of a game instantly. A moment's work of this calibre from him, perhaps at the edge of his own penalty area, could take his side out of an alarming defensive situation and have it menacing the other goal immediately. I saw him do this once against Liverpool and the moment stunned that ferocious crowd into silence.

Charlton makes his own rules for dealing with a football. He is a player to admire but not for younger ones to copy. When he strikes the ball he often has his head up high, instead of looking down over the ball as the coaches teach. He will flick at it with the outside of his left foot when leaning back looking at the sky. When players on his own side are unaccustomed to him they often find that the ball comes to them, having miraculously been 'bent' round some obstructing opponent, spinning violently and therefore difficult to control; only the best can take advantage of such passes, as Denis Law, Best and Jimmy Greaves (in the international side) all have. Charlton does not dribble with the ball in the sense that Best does, patting it between his feet, nor does he run with it as if it is tied by elastic to him, as in the case of Pele, of Brazil, so that it bounces against his knees, thighs, stomach, ankles as he moves. Charlton kicks the ball close to the ground in front of him, often a long way in front, and runs like a sprinter behind it, almost as if there was no ball at all. No boy could possibly be taught such a method of playing football.

This run deceives defenders. They see the ball coming towards them, with Charlton well behind it, and they think they can reach it before him. Suddenly, just as they commit themselves, his right shoulder dips, his whole weight goes momentarily on his right foot, flat on the grass, and then he has sped past them the other way, kicking the ball in front of him as he goes. His own speed, coupled with the defender's impetus, often means that he is ten yards clear before the defender has turned. To be beaten by Charlton's swerve is to be beaten for good. If the defender anticipates the swerve and turns in the right direction Charlton will clear the tackle expertly like a hurdler.

There is delicious exhilaration in watching movement like this. Crowds will him to repeat it, and if he gets the ball and pauses as if gathering himself for such a run the whole sound of the stadium changes from its baying or grumbling into an excited purr. If he decides the moment is not right, and releases the ball quickly with a merely sensible short pass, there is a deep groan of disappointment.

He has his bad matches, when his touch deserts him and the casual flicks and lobs skim away erratically, sometimes presenting the other team with the initiative they had lost. In games like these his shooting at goal can be laughably wild, and yet there is seldom laughter; the communal embarrassment is the same that settles around a wrong final note from the recital platform. Charlton hates these lapses. He reacts to them with something close to self-revulsion, like a man discovering a flea in his vest. He shakes his head wretchedly, apologizes to the company, and on his very worst days may keep clear of the ball for a while. More often he tries to compose himself, trapping the ball and striking it with an unusual, elaborate care. It is only now that he looks awkward. When Charlton is keeping his eye intently on the ball, as every good player is supposed to, then he is at his least effective. He is not a player's player, in the sense of being reliable, even though he is entirely professional in his attitude to the game; he is certainly a spectator's player, in the sense that he is a sight to watch.

His dejection in failure, even in the momentary kind, is more easily understood when Charlton has been met off the field. There is a natural diffidence in him, a sense of anxiety not to show himself up in public. His shyness was brought home to me first of all when he was 21, unmarried and living in lodgings. I had some fairly harmless questions to ask him for the newspaper I was working for at the time, and the whole interview was conducted on the doorstep, with Charlton holding on to the doorknob, not being in the least obstructive but blushing and leaving words trailing indistinctly and ambiguously in the air. He said at the time that he had always found it hard to answer any questions about himself. Seven years later, when he was a much better player and going bald, he was still far from casual in conversation even in his own home, only showing a marked step forward in self-confidence when he was holding one of his children in his arms. He has done a good deal of talking to youth clubs and at sports clubs functions in recent years, yet there was a distinct nerviness in his voice when I heard him deliver a few impromptu sentences in a hospital's broadcast at half-time in one of Liverpool's midweek matches. He smokes more than would be expected of a man who is still one of the fastest movers in international football in spite of being 30 years old.

He gets the star footballer's profusion of flattery. His name is chanted to raise the spirits of ticket queues in the rain; vivid, coarse girls have to be held off by policemen when he gets in and out of the Manchester United coach; small boys write him letters of charming clumsiness and kick footballs with his autograph on them; he has been European Footballer of the Year, and a poll of referees has voted him Model Player. His wife is pretty, so are his two daughters, and he lives in a rich man's house in a rich man's neighbourhood. He is the classic working-class hero who has made it to glamour and Nob Hill.

Charlton's childhood was spent in Ashington, Northumberland, and he was a miner's son, living in one of those immensely long, pitshaft-straight rows of houses which characterize the area. Classically, for a workers' hero, he owes much to his mother.

Mrs Elizabeth Charlton is a grey-haired, handsome woman now. It is said in Ashington that when she was a girl she could dribble with a football as well as most of the boys. She was born into football and she knew the game and its ways as theatre mums know make-up and stage-doors. Her father was a goalkeeper, called 'Tanner' Milburn, and her four brothers were all fullbacks with League clubs, the Milburns, Jack, George, Jimmy and Stan. The greatest of all the Milburns, the centre-forward 'Wor Jackie', of Newcastle United and England, is her cousin. The story goes that when her eldest son (Jack Charlton, Leeds' and England's centre-half) first made her a grandmother she was asked by a friend in the street how the baby was, and she answered: 'Eee, the bairn's lovely. And his feet are fine, too.'

When Mrs Charlton talks about her sons her face takes on a brightness which strips the years away. One can see where Bobby got that exuberance of movement. She told me that when the two boys were babies – Jack is the older by eighteen months – she used to take them in one pram to Ashington's matches. She said: 'I used to leave them behind the dressing-rooms, and whenever the crowd roared they'd jump.'

Bobby went to a local primary school, which then as now was a hideous line of apexes in blood-red brick. There is a long, rectangular playground where the boys play football in engrossed tangles, their faces set fiercely against defeat. It was here that Bobby wore his first football strip, a set of maroon shirts with black shorts which were made out of wartime blackout curtaining by one of the women teachers. The school still has the set. Bobby was captain of the team which won the

East Northumberland junior schools league championship
wearing it. These matters are not taken lightly in Ashington.

The headmaster at the time was Mr James Hamilton, and I
talked to him in his bed-sitter when he was nearing 80 and in
retirement. He had a photograph on one wall of Bobby and
some thirty other small boys with their arms folded across their
chests. That was Bobby Charlton as school captain, he said.
'He didn't mention that in his book. He was too modest.' He
produced another photograph of an unmistakable Charlton,
at 11 years old, holding a trophy in the middle of his football
team. Mr Hamilton is on one flank of the group and the sports
master, Mr Norman McGuiness, on the other. Mr Hamilton
said that when Bobby got through his scholarship examination
for senior school he was directed to Morpeth Grammar School.
He said: 'It's one of those snooty schools where they play rugby.
We got him transferred to the grammar school at Bedlington.'

Both Charlton and his mother say that Mr McGuiness
contributed more than anyone else to Bobby's development as
a young footballer. I met him at the secondary school where
he was now headmaster, a small, tightly made man of 52 with
some alarming stories of contemporary adolescent indiscipline.
He sounded glad to be able to talk about someone who had
responded more readily to him; but he confessed he taught
Charlton little, merely encouraged him. He said: 'There
really wasn't much he could be coached in. My first memory of
him is seeing this small, thin lad of 9 playing football with the
14-year-olds and just waltzing through them. It didn't take a
Solomon to see he had natural ability. Even at nine he had
a body swerve and a natural check that would take the other
man the wrong way.'

Mr McGuiness clearly had enjoyed running junior schoolboy
football, its sudden revelations of talent delighting him, the

general enthusiasm having its own charm and calling for special bending of the rules. He said that even then Charlton could hit the ball as strongly as the seniors, and his side used to win heavily. He said: 'But, you know, the thing was never to let the scores get too big. The unwritten law was that you didn't let anyone get into double figures. After a certain stage of the game, if one side was winning easily, you just whistled everyone offside the moment they got into the penalty area.'

This was serious stuff, nevertheless. Mr McGuiness used to put his 10- and 11-year-olds through six-a-side games in the playground after school three times a week. There was no resistance to the training. Then as now, as the current head-master of Charlton's primary school said to me, Ashington boys were 'football daft'.

There was less devotion to football at Bedlington Grammar School, and the prompting hand which put Charlton in the game as a career still came from Ashington. The headmaster of the secondary school which Jack Charlton was attending was a remarkable man. Mr Stuart Hemingway came to approve of professional football, rejecting the prejudice he had held against it in his younger days, when he went to Ashington in the twenties. He had been a Foundation Scholar at Manchester Grammar School, he was steeped in church music, and he thought that education was the key to the emancipation of the unemployed working-classes. In Ashington they taught him that football was.

He too was in retirement when I met him, a thin, keen-faced man in his 70s, with sharp wit in spite of a wavering voice. He had been years ahead of his time as an educationist. He introduced foreign languages, and even school trips abroad, to a colliers' non-selective secondary school.

He remembered the sad deprivation of the Northumberland

mining areas between the wars. He said: 'That was terrible poverty. In the summer the boys used to come to school in their bare feet to save their boots for winter – and for football. I was always against the professional game. I was against this chasing after schoolboys to turn them into footballers. Then I came to realize that this professional football was nothing bad at all. It was something good for them. It could be work. I think the footballer's wage then was about £4 a week.'

Once he had taken his boys out of the local schools league, to protect them from the tough competition which put the most talented ones into the public eye. Now he urged them into competitions so that they should not be overlooked.

He had played inside-right for Manchester University, and he retained his affection for the club he had watched in his boyhood, Manchester United. By the time the Charlton brothers were in their teens he was well versed in the ways by which professional clubs picked up young players, and with Bobby he stole a march on the clubs' scouts. Soon after Bobby's 15th birthday he wrote to Busby at United. He had already advised Mr and Mrs Charlton that United was the best club for their younger son. Mr Hemingway, talking about Charlton as a boy player, used exactly the word that Mrs Charlton used when she remembered the excitement of watching him play. They both said: 'He used to *delight* people.'

Mrs Charlton, meanwhile, had been doing some coaching of her own. She and Mr McGuiness were determined that Bobby should get into the England schoolboys team. She said: 'The one thing we worried about was that he was slow off the mark.' She was handling the teapot, which is always handy for visitors to her house, and she jabbed it about the air to emphasize her point. 'I talked to Mr McGuiness about it and he said if we could quicken him up over 30 yards he'd be all right.

Well, I asked ever so many men around here to take the job
on, but they wouldn't. So I took him down to the park myself
and got him doing sprints.'

It is an appealing picture: the fair boy and the brisk, pretty
mother, she pacing out the distances and urging him shrilly on,
a few bystanders nodding at each other and agreeing that
'Tanner' Milburn's lass would have her lad in the England team
if anybody could. She said, smiling in hindsight at the humour
in the situation: 'It was 20 yards, then back; 80 yards, back
again.' Now she laughed outright. 'I don't know if it helped,
but Bobby got his cap,' she said.

Manchester United's chief scout, Joe Armstrong, a stocky,
trundly old man now, with a round, lined face and wispy hair,
watched Bobby Charlton play for East Northumberland
schoolboys against Hebburn and Jarrow boys on February 9,
1953. He would remember the day until he died, he said. 'It
was a thin morning, with frost on the ground, and we were
peering through the mist. Ooh, I can see it all now.' He winced
at the memory of the cold. 'Bobby didn't do so much that day,
but it was enough for me.'

There was also a scout from the Sunderland club at the game.
Mrs Charlton remembered that Bobby was disappointed
because, after the match, this man went to speak to the goalkeeper on his side but not to him. She said: 'But then Joe came
up, and he said, "I don't want to butter you up, Missis, but
your boy will play for England before he's 21."'

Mrs Charlton was informative about the way professional
football clubs hunt for young players. She said that once it
was known that Manchester United had made contact other
clubs had representatives calling at the house almost daily.
She said: 'They were offering us the world. One fellow offered
£800. Another said he'd double whatever was the highest offer

we'd had. He didn't even ask what it was. There was another fellow in the front room who said he'd got £550 in his brief-case, and we could have it there and then.'

All these inducements were illegal, but the practice was widespread. Ashington was not appalled by it all, but the Charltons were properly suspicious. Mrs Charlton said: 'Jackie Milburn told us not to be taken in by anyone. He said, "They'll all offer you the earth, but even if you say yes you might never get it."' The scouts' persistence brought them to the house at all times of the day and night. Mrs Charlton said: 'I'd be cleaning the fireplace in the morning and I'd look round and there'd be another one standing behind me. There were times when we've had one in the front room and one in the kitchen.'

Eventually there were eighteen clubs asking for Bobby's signature. Joe Armstrong kept close to the family, and sometimes he had his wife with him. The education authorities were objecting to the retinue of scouts now following Bobby to every school match he played. Mrs Charlton said: 'Bobby had already decided it was going to be Manchester United. Joe had come first, you see. Joe used to say at the matches he was Bobby's uncle, and then he'd introduce his wife and say, "And this is his Auntie Sally."'

Busby saw Charlton play for the first time at a public trial for the England schoolboys' side at Manchester City's ground, and he decided he wanted him. Charlton left Ashington for Manchester in July 1953.

Nowadays a boy can join a professional club as an apprentice at 15, and if he does not match up to expectations he can revert to amateur status later on. But this was not the case in the fifties. As Charlton put it: 'You either went on the ground staff and spent your time cleaning toilets, or you went to work.' He took a job in an engineering works close to Old Trafford until he was 17, when he could sign as a professional. For a while he played in a youth side which used to win, against opponents trying to impress the United representatives on the touchline, by scores like 12–0 regularly. He said the experience taught him how to take rough treatment. His first League game came in the month of his 19th birthday, and he scored twice. As Joe Armstrong had forecast, he played for England before he was 21.

Drama and gloss come to every star footballer, and Charlton has had more than most. He has travelled in a score of different countries, and he is accustomed to the pampering that surrounds valuable human cargoes in transit. Yet his wife says that every time he drives past a particular hotel in Sale, near Manchester, he points it out and tells her it was the first hotel he ever stayed in. He was 15 at the time, and where Charlton came from boys might have seen the insides of off-licences but not of hotels, where people ate and slept. He said to me, his Geordie accent still clear: 'Well, at school that was the end. I mean, that was really something.' It was the first time, he said, he was conscious of being looked at.

Charlton was in the Munich air crash, and got out of it unhurt. He was playing for United soon afterwards. He has always said that it had no lasting effect on him, although it is difficult to believe that the shock did not linger. He played for England in the year of the disaster, and he has been in the national side ever since. For all that, it is true to say that it took him until his mid-twenties to find the authority of personality to complement and extend his abounding talents. Busby says that is because the great years of a player's career are those between the ages of 26 and 32. No one can speak with more knowledge.

In the 1967–8 season I have seen less ease in Charlton's game than there was three seasons ago, but more wisdom and a new sense of responsibility. The sparse hair flops across the bald crown; the face is tauter than ever. No one can play eleven years of top quality football at his pace without showing the strain. But his speed still astonishes spectators and opponents. He can chase opposing, younger forwards from behind, make up a ten-yard gap and get in front of them to force them into parting with the ball. He is one of the very few players who can bring rheumy-eyed sportswriters to their feet in a press box. He has not been staled by knocks or mud or the dragging weight of repetition. He does not make a crowd think murder; what he gives them is delight.

2 The Manager

A notably frank and intelligent study of the Svengali figure of
football, the manager, published in the FA Year Book for
1965–6, contained this wry comment: 'At the moment a
manager or team manager can be appointed in rather vague
circumstances.' It is just as true to say that the circumstances of
a manager's dismissal, often euphemistically called 'resignation',
are usually equally opaque. We are not talking about the basic
reason for a club's getting rid of one man and taking on
another; that is to be found obviously enough in a club's lack
of success. But there is illogic in the moments of arrival and
departure. Some managers stay for years with a club without
winning it a thing to decorate the boardroom walls, then
suddenly the axe falls and the new man arrives with a solemn
assurance of the directors' support for every new measure.
There can be few simultaneous victors in football, and managers
are as insecure as a 1–0 lead.

The trouble with the football manager's job is that an
important part of the essence of football is insecurity. It is the
uncertainty in sport which gives it much of its drama. The
emergence of new talent, an unexpected surge of resolve, a
cohering of previously disparate abilities, a little luck: all these
things can overturn established form. This season's puzzled-
looking losers can be fluent winners next year. This month's
knowing maturity can sink into the ponderousness of the

overaged by the time of the return match. The manager lives on hope as well as on his shrewdness, his club's resources and his self-confidence. In the end he is the sum of his results, and his problem is that while he can develop players, buy talent, drive and coax and plan, he is powerless during the game. Disaffected players can ruin him, unless he can convince his directors of his paramount importance.

Not many managers can do that. The running of the majority of professional football clubs remains firmly in the hands of amateurs: of directors who are often obsessed football fans but who have never known the game from where it really counts, on the field in the toughest competition. They look at football differently from the way the professionals see it. They are superfans, anxious for success because it makes them feel better, because it makes them socially enviable, because it nourishes their own ego and that of the community in which they are luminaries. The professional derives pleasure from these things as well, but he is involved with deeper satisfactions and desolation. He knows when he has tried and been let down by inadequate ability or effort around him; he knows when he has been beaten through his own limitations, and when he has succeeded by compensating for them at great personal cost. He is aware that he knows more than the amateurs but also that he exists only because of them. The professional is closer to the opposing professionals than to the amateurs on his own side. His approach is contained in one question which he asks himself over and again: How can I win? To him method is vital, not just extremely interesting as it is to those who only watch.

The most successful contemporary managers – Busby, Bill Shankly at Liverpool, Ramsey, Don Revie at Leeds, Bill Nicholson at Tottenham – have all been top-quality players in the past. But fine players do not necessarily make the most effective managers. The most arresting recent example has been Billy Wright's brief, troubled experience as manager of Arsenal. Even Wright's reputation as a deeply respected captain of the England team could not overcome a breakdown in understanding in the triangle of boardroom, manager and players. Raich Carter, a brilliantly gifted player who could impose his will on a game, did not make the same impact as a manager.

Personality must be the key factor in managerial success. It is not a question of being a nice man or a nasty one, of being likeable or aloof, of being imaginative or cautious, hard or indulgent in discipline. All of these things are subordinate to the essential quality that, it seems, all the most successful managers have: the capacity to dominate. This is not just an overbearing manner, a thrusting of two fists at the world; it is not just arrogance. It is a steeliness in a man's make-up, the will to make his methods tell. He is the kind of man who will not permit interference by the amateurs, and the kind who will never be invited to work for a board not prepared to be over-shadowed. The successful manager may have all kinds of talents, from charm to low cunning, but to stay successful he needs to be very close to indomitable.

The turnover in Football League managers is notoriously heavy, and it tells its own story. On average since the end of the Second World War 25 per cent of them a year have changed jobs. This reflects the tensions in professional football, the anxiety for success which grips directors. But it reflects too the failure of the managers, as a group, to establish their authority in the sport. Alan Brown, Sunderland's manager, has put it more strongly than I have ever heard from anyone else. Managers, he told me, were treated 'with the contempt they

D

deserve'. The ambition of individuals, yet also their moral weakness, has brought about that lack of will among managers as a body which leaves them defenceless against the amateurs. They have yet to find the sense of community interest and self-respect which won the players their freedom of movement and their right to negotiate an honest contract for their talents. The managers have no concerted voice. The best of them can command the dignity of a contract; most work week-to-week, perhaps well paid but subject to the whims, the irritability, the explosions of frustration of the grocers, the solicitors and the builders' merchants in the boardroom.

That is why the manager's personality is so important. If he cannot deter uninformed, truculent criticism by his presence, and has to spend much of his time in club politics, flattering here, ingratiating there, he is like a centre-forward with a hamstring gone; the harder he tries the more he damages himself. This is to put the matter at its extreme, of course. Between the most respected, successful managers and the ill-equipped kind who flit from one club to another for a few opportunist years, before giving up for good and settling for the used car trade or the dance hall business, there is the solid core of men who speak their minds, accept that they are not wholly in charge and compromise in honest reluctance. Now and again they get close to winning something exciting.

Of course, what a club wants when it looks for a new manager is not always an inspirational talent which will win the FA Cup or the League championship. The term 'success' may mean the revival of a club which has sunk down to the bottom of one of the lower divisions, or the boosting of spirit in another lodged stubbornly in the lower half of the first. Boldness, even ruthlessness, may be the vital characteristic for a manager acquired for such a job. Because of the weight of confidence it puts on the directors, and the likely cost of the exercise if the manager fails, the man needs courage and flair.

Two instances, involving very different men, illustrate the size of the job and the differing ways in which it can be tackled. Tony Waddington took over as manager of Stoke City when he was 34, which is unusually young for the task, and when Stoke were rooted firmly in the Second Division and playing to a dispirited, sparse crowd. Waddington is a calm, worldly man who talks as if he expects other adults to know that the human race does not live entirely by the Scouts code of conduct. I remember his telling me in 1966 that other clubs had done much of his work for him. The point was that he piloted Stoke back into Division One by some extremely astute buying and selling of players. He said: 'Let me put it like this. You don't sit down at the start of the season and say, "I hope so-and-so gets kicked out by his club." But it's just happened that the right players have come available when we needed them.'

But how skilfully and with what timing they were bought. The romantic element in football, the appeal to the emotions, is just as strong as the cold acumen in it. Waddington's first acquisition was Stanley Matthews, and this was as irresistible an appeal as has ever been made to a town's football followers. Matthews had been the darling of Stoke City as a boy player and then as one of the world's most extraordinary virtuosi. He returned to Stoke from Blackpool, more than ten years older than his new manager. Waddington put the situation tersely enough. 'The point about Stoke,' he said, 'was that everyone had been saying for years that when things got desperate Stan would come back. The Messiah would come and rescue us. But we'd been waiting so long no one really believed it any more.'

The lapsed fans trooped dutifully back. Waddington pursued his policy of buying mature, famous players on whose specialized talents he knew he could rely. Again the appeal was not just in the men's football; most of them struck chords in the fans' hearts of their own younger days. The roll-call was like the top table of some Old Masters reunion dinner: Matthews, Eddie Stuart, Eddie Clamp, Dennis Viollet, Jimmy McIlroy, Maurice Setters, George Eastham, Peter Dobing, Roy Vernon. The Press played up to the ploy delightedly, with affectionate jokes about Old Contemptibles and Stoke Pensioners, and references to teachers' spankings for younger teams. Waddington proved an excellent public relations man, which is a quality a number of the best managers share. He never overstated his team's performances, never whined when he lost. The publicity was sometimes embarrassing, as when Stoke lost 6-0 when McIlroy, freshly joined from Burnley, played his first game for his new club; but Stoke were being talked about; the damaging silence was gone for good.

Waddington spent a quarter of a million pounds on players in his first seven years as Stoke's manager; but he also recouped £100,000 on sales of players. He has not yet won any major honour for his club, beyond getting them up out of Division Two; but that is enough to establish his value, and he has a long-term contract. He runs the club like a small business which is turning out craftsmen's products, not expecting to have to immerse himself in his players' private lives, as some managers with younger teams must. He is neither soft nor cynical, but he has no compunction about getting rid of a player when he regards him as obsolete. His buying of Gordon Banks, England's goalkeeper and arguably the best in the world, was as important a contribution to self-preservation as the acquiring of Matthews was to initial impetus. Waddington is a professional.

So, in a different style, is Don Revie, who became manager of Leeds United in 1961, making an immediate switch from being a player. Revie's nature has less urbanity and more urgency than Waddington's. He is very much a players' manager, often in his tracksuit, demonstrating and criticizing and encouraging by example. His firm views on how managers should relate their abilities and ambitions to the players' own personalities were formed in his own long and distinguished playing career.

The only manager he ever fully admired was the first one he played for, Johnny Duncan of Leicester City. He was a restless man after he left Leicester, moving to Hull, Manchester City and Sunderland before joining Leeds. He was one of the early exploiters of the deep-lying, scheming centre-forward role, disrupting opposing defences by dragging the centre-half about the field in his wake, spraying passes to the wings, always busy, very intent. But though highly talented he was seldom content with the treatment he got from clubs; his years as a player were marked by controversy. When he became a manager he was determined that his own players would at least not be subjected to the slights and the managerial indifference which he remembered as common to some clubs in his day as a player. He knew well enough what could either depress or stimulate players. No one in Revie's club would ever have to wait for Friday night's local newspaper to find out whether he was in the first team or not.

He took over what he described to me as 'a dead club'. He said: 'There were players here who didn't care whether they played or not. I got rid of twenty-seven in two years.' He concentrated in the first place on lifting the pall of despondency which hung about the place, and to do this he changed the strip to a streamlined all-white, which added a psychological fillip, and followed that by introducing new training kit, even a new style of boots; he insisted that the team, when travelling to away matches, had to stay in the best hotels available. 'I said from now on we had to eat off the *à la carte* and not the straight menu.' He increased the scouting staff heavily. The directors, backing the new enthusiasm, gave parties for the players to show they were interested in them. It was a kind of workers' revolt, and in the short term it was costly. The club finished the 1961-2 season with a loss of £72,000 and went close to being relegated to Division Three.

But Revie's concern was not for quick success. He was trying to build firmly. He knew the kind of club he wanted, and he had the strength of will not to be deflected in his purpose. He built a young, tenacious defence around Jack Charlton, and in doing it upgraded Charlton's own play to the standard which made him England's centre-half. He spent little at first on new players, openly naming Busby's ability to find and develop the very young as the example he proposed to follow. Success, once it began, was a considerable harvest of near misses. The club got back into Division One in 1964 and reached the FA Cup Final the year after, when they were also runners-up in the League championship. They were championship runners-up again in 1966, and in 1967 lost to Zagreb in the final of the Fairs Cup. Crowds for home matches are now frequently around 40,000. Late in the 1967-8 season Leeds won their first trophy under Revie's management, the Football League Cup.

Revie's concern for the players' welfare has not diminished since his early months as a manager. He has pressed home his plans for producing players from his own nursery, which he conducts with the closest possible attention to the worries and uncertainties of youth. Junior players are taught carefully about bank accounts, table manners and sex. There are regular homilies about 'keeping their hair short and their clothes smart and not getting caught up with loose girls'. Revie listens patiently to a variety of bewildered players on the tricky subjects of 'the motor car, the house, the mother-in-law or the wife.' Directors advise on the safe and profitable ways of investing money. When the team is on tour, or playing away from home in England, the accompanying staff goes watchfully through the vacated bedrooms, looking for overlooked personal belongings like matron at boarding school. Footballers were often helpless off the field, Revie remembers, and the increasing tension of the sport makes this kind of practical helping hand more necessary nowadays, not less.

Revie's attitude towards football is still that of a passionate player. He is a big, flat-fronted man with an outdoors face as if he lives permanently in a keen wind. When he talks about prickly matters, such as dirty play or players' rough words to referees, he always emphasizes the player's case – not just on behalf of Leeds' players, but for the professionals in general. Billy Bremner, his captain, has been often in trouble with referees, and Revie defends him, not by refusing to admit the player's mistakes but by pointing to the courage and the talent which counter-balance them. Also, he adds, Bremner has not always been as guilty as the less excitable, more calculating players who have provoked him. That is a professional's voice, not an apologist's.

The football manager is essentially a manager of people. I hope to get closer to his job and his method with character studies of five managers, each of them markedly an individual, all with the common characteristic of a compelling will.

1 *Stan Cullis (and persistence)*

A footballer's first manager is bound to influence him greatly.
Stan Cullis's formative years in professional football were spent
under Major Buckley, probably the most autocratic manager
League football has had in the last fifty years. It is hardly likely,
in fact, that his special brand of squire-like management could
ever be repeated. Cullis remembers him as 'a one-man band,
a man who knew exactly what he wanted and where he was
going'. When Cullis says that Buckley was 'never one of these
equivocal people', he could as well be talking about himself.
Cullis has a name in the sport for making sure that players
know to the letter what he expects from them, and whether he
thinks he is getting it.

Cullis's playing career was informed always by his implacable
character. It showed in his stance over a ball: an intent crouch
with his bald forehead jutting belligerently forward and his
elbows crooked away from his sides. He seldom allowed himself
a careless contact with the ball. I was a boy when he was
England's and Wolves' captain, and his is the figure I most
readily associate with the term 'centre-half'. He defined the
position for me, not just by the way he went crushingly into a
tackle or hit a long pass firmly – a captain's unquestionable
instruction – to one of his wingers: it was the sternness of the
man himself which fixed the role. Being a centre-half is an
austere responsibility, which permits no frivolous embellish-
ments of manner. (There have been some centre-halves who
have had bullying, even vicious, natures; I cannot think of a
petulant one.)

The Second World War interrupted Cullis's career, and he
stopped playing soon after it. He had been a precociously

advanced player, and now he became the youngest manager in the League. He took over Wolves when he was 32. The changes in attitude to the game, which were shortly to increase its speed and its overall cleverness, taking the advantage away from the heavier men, were already apparent. As an adolescent professional Cullis had been trained largely on aids to stamina, with a lot of work in the gymnasium on the punchbag and with the medicine ball, and out of doors a great deal of lapping round the pitch. Some of the equipment had a makeshift quality: for instance, a 'heading machine' which was just a suspended ball, the footballer's equivalent of the boxer's speedball. Training with a football had much emphasis on developing 'the wrong foot', the one the player preferred not to kick with. Cullis introduced a greater concentration on the use of the ball in training, which is nowadays as much a part of the basis of the preparation of a professional side as is the mere development of fitness.

But physical resilience has always been of prime importance to Cullis's teams. Wolves have always had one of the most punishing, pre-season stamina courses in the game, and under Cullis no player who could not overcome it could expect to make the first team. It involved a full-pelt run up a steep hill in part of the tangled heathland of Cannock Chase, and it has a reputation in British football like the assault course at Eaton Hall used to have among army subalterns.

Wolves set the pace of English football under Cullis, their success dramatic and continuing. They won the FA Cup in 1949 and 1960, and they were the League champions in 1954, 1958 and 1959. They were Britain's representatives in European club football. They excited the same kind of following by the fans and the Press that Tottenham Hotspur commanded in the early 1960s and which Manchester United have secured during the last dozen years. But Cullis's direction created a different kind of football from the mixture of general calm and personal brilliance which has been the hallmark of the other two clubs. Cullis's teams represented all that was most dramatic and most effective in the game he had matured in. It was a simpler method than United's or Spurs', involving hard-running wingers who could score goals, strength and industry in mid-field and a big, brave centre-forward. It was a team of well-drilled, skilled workers of great heart, extremely hard to contain while they were in full cry, limited by their specialization once they began to lose their edge.

Cullis is entirely frank about that period. He said to me: 'The team I had possibly didn't match the Spurs side which won the championship in terms of skill. But if we were deficient there, we made up for it with fitness and successful tactics.' But regardless of the manner of the success, the fifties for Wolves and for Cullis were, as he put it, 'Glory, glory hallelujah'. In 1960 no manager looked more secure, and none more personally popular with supporters. He had never been associated with any other club. A nod in the street from Stan Cullis was not something to be quickly forgotten.

But once a team begins to slide, overtaken by its own age and others' sudden flowering, past success is only briefly a glad memory; it quickly becomes an accusing finger. As Cullis put it, with some bitterness: 'Looking back, I'd only created a yardstick that people could criticize me against.' By 1962 Wolves were 18th in Division One, in 1964 16th, and now there were ominous stories in circulation of recrimination inside the club. In the following year Cullis was suddenly no longer manager; Wolves were relegated to Division Two.

This passage of events shows plainly enough how insecure a manager's position is. Even a man of proved ability is only as safe as his directors allow him to be. Cullis told me that there came a point when the composition of the board was such that he knew his days were numbered. 'I knew it was only a question of time,' he said.

From the vantage point of hindsight he considered what he might have done to have arrested his team's decline, and his uncertainty on the question drummed home the manager's dilemma. At what point does he introduce new blood? There is no point in tinkering with a winning side; but if he is acute and resolutely critical enough, can a manager spot the impending collapse of a player's game before its damage is done? What's more, a team is a blend, and a breakdown in one position can immediately reduce the related power of another. Cullis seemed to be blaming himself, although not with complete conviction, for not following firmly the maxim he now applies in his management of Birmingham: 'You must remember you're dependent on what eleven players do on the field. I must have players who will always give 100 per cent effort. On the basis of survival, once I see there's a part of the team not fully functioning I must get rid of it and fill that place with someone who will work.'

He joined Birmingham, who were relegated to Division Two at the same time as Wolves, after several months out of football. When I talked to him in 1967 he had good reason for his vigorous display of self-confidence. It was the knowing, non-illusory kind that a man of 50 with triumph and dejection behind him deserves. When he first took over at Birmingham the club was in the bottom four of Division Two, and playing to home crowds of around 12,000. But he had finished the 1966–7 season in tenth place and with an average gate of nearly 20,000. I asked him if he felt any bitterness towards the Wolves boardroom, and he said: 'Put it this way. Nothing would give me greater pleasure than to take my team there in the First Division and beat them.'

While he was out of football he wrote about the game for the *News of the World*, which took him frequently to the paper's London office. He had received letters of sympathy and intimations of goodwill from people who were apparently only casually interested in the sport but outraged by what seemed to be injustice, and also from lifelong Wolves fans; but one Saturday night in London he had an encounter which illustrates something of the fierceness with which people involve themselves in football. He said: 'I was walking away from the office, and a man stopped me. He was a Londoner. He said, "You're Stan Cullis, aren't you?" He said, "Me and my wife are Arsenal supporters. Do you know what? When Arsenal are playing away we can't wait to find out how they've got on. But the next thing we look for is to see how Wolves went on. If they've lost we say that's good, and we go out and have a drink. What they did to you was shocking."'

Cullis told me that story with a flat detachment, not with any discernible rancour, after we had been discussing the compulsion of the game for people brought up to it. He was making the point that when football followers see something which offends them they direct their anger not on the individuals concerned but on the club as a whole. A dirty player, for example, means a dirty-playing club to them; an outstandingly brilliant forward makes them see his club in a brighter, more glamorous light. More damage to the game can be done by individual acts of vindictiveness than the guilty realize, or the game deserves.

Cullis still looks much as he used to on the field. I always saw him as a bald man, so that his almost total baldness is no surprise; he is not greatly heavier; the voice is much lighter than the personality. He talks with less solemnity about the game than many managers; he is anxious, it seemed to me, not to immerse his emotional self into the game so deeply that he cannot use his tactician's eye. 'I've lived with tension, dear me!' he said, the inoffensive little expletive reminding me of his puritan's reputation for never swearing. 'You create that yardstick with success, and every time you win that heightens the tension for you again.' He knew there were managers who seldom showed their anxiety; he was convinced there was not one who did not have it.

His comments on the status of the manager in the game as a whole were coldly amused. 'We are regarded as coming from the uneducated classes,' he said. 'The League and the FA keep discussing the game, keep asking themselves how they can improve it, but they've never sought the advice of the professionals. In terms of status we've made very little progress over the years.'

As with the total professional in most fields, there is more insight than sentimentality in Cullis's view of the game as it used to be played and as it now challenges him. The training of players is far more imaginative, he said, and it has produced a much higher general standard than he knew as a young player. But the basic principle that extreme physical fitness created a vital self-confidence was as true now as it ever had been, he said. 'The first thing I set out to do when I joined Birmingham was to convince the players they were better than they thought they were.'

Cullis believes in persistence, not just for its moral worth but also because he sees logical advantage in it: the more times his forwards shoot at goal the more opportunities there are for the opposing goalkeeper to miss the ball. Cullis does not order his football in pretty packages; he likes it to have substance and to travel fast. He says of players that they come in two general kinds: those whose attitude to a manager's advice is that it is probably intended to help, and those who assume that it is carping criticism. 'As long as a player believes the manager is trying to improve him you're in with a chance,' he said. 'Unfortunately you've got certain players who are like a lot of women – all advice upsets them.'

He thought that the new influence of extensive educational attainment which some young players brought to football nowadays was more of a help than a hindrance, although it made no contribution at all to the forlorn task of trying to develop a player beyond his gifts. 'You've got to assess their IQ,' he said. 'With some players you can get your message across just by telling them. With others you've got to do it by repetition in training, over and over again. With them you can't get technical and expect them to understand. But it's a myth that you can take a university lad and educate him in football twice as quickly. He'll only get there quicker if he and the duller lad both have the same level of football skill. You can have dim men who have an instinct for the game. They can appreciate things on a football field that are too intricate for the university lad.'

Cullis still believes strongly that only work brings success in the end. He sees no likelihood of fact in the romantic proposition of the indolent player who can explode a dazzling performance before the crowd on an instant, summoning the strength of muscle and purpose which he has been concealing from the world all the week. 'Players condition themselves for Saturday,' said Cullis. 'There are some who think they can freewheel during the week, and then just turn it on. It's a myth.'

Cullis's conviction that players tell most of what he needs to know about them in training is not shared by some other managers. But they deal more in flair and individual invention. Cullis has no wish to subdue either in his players. But he knows that they do not always go with constant honesty of effort, and his experience has taught him that he dare not rely on anything less.

2 *Alan Brown (and absolute trust)*

Alan Brown filled a gap of disappointment in his early life by becoming a policeman. It is intriguing to speculate on where he would now have been in the police hierarchy if the pull of football had not been so strong that it tugged him back into the game. He would surely have been one of the major scourges of the criminal classes, irresistible in his contempt for corruption. I cannot help thinking that football's gain was crime's as well.

Brown was the man who restored public confidence and self-respect at the Sunderland club in the late fifties after a spectacular scandal over illegal payments. 'If you like, I cleaned it up,' he says. His cold, sorry anger in the face of greed and irregularity in matters of money is one of the institutions of British football. The fact that it is common knowledge that parents and boys are sometimes persuaded towards a particular club by costly gifts does not sway his attitude in the least. He said to me: 'On two occasions parents have said to me, when I came to the point of signing their lads, "Well, what about a bit of so and so?" My reply was, "Look, you can take your boy home if you like, but he won't get anything illegal here." Then they said, "Well, what about a suit of clothes for the lad?" I replied, "If and when he goes abroad with us he'll get his blazer and flannels like everybody else."'

When Sheffield Wednesday reached the Cup Final under his management in 1966 the players were much aggrieved when Brown resolutely squashed their lobbying for more tickets than the figure laid down by the FA as the players' allocation. 'The fact is,' he said, 'that the clubs and the players don't get enough tickets. But the thing to do is to change the rules, not break them. I said I would rather leave my job than break the rule. It was not my business that other clubs would have given way. How does a man manage if he hasn't got courage and responsibility?'

Brown says with a smile that has something of the sense of personal hurt in it that the newspapers have tagged him for ever as 'The Iron Man'. He said: 'I think everywhere I've been I've been viewed at the start with distaste.' His first post as a manager was at Burnley, where he had played centre-half a few years before. 'The first greeting I got was to hear on the grapevine that four of the well-known players had said, "If yon So-and-so comes here I'm in for a transfer".' But Brown's avowed commitment to the moral values, such as truth and frankness, made absolute by his joining of Moral Rearmament when he was in Sunderland, leads him to acquit the Press of outright distortion of his character. 'I think people miss a lot of warmth in a man when they don't really know him,' he said. 'But I'll concede that in the end, over the years, the right picture comes through.'

There are many honest men in football, but Brown is fiercely attached to protecting integrity in the game as its central factor. It is more important to him than brilliance; success without it is to him merely deceit. His first value to football, which may not be of total satisfaction to his directors or his team's supporters, is that he is one of the counter-balances to the utter ruthlessness elsewhere in the game. If every team was conducted as Brown conducts his there would be less drama, less thrill, less interest in football; if every team was run as some other managers run theirs there would eventually be no sport in the business at all.

Brown does not produce dull sides; he built the Burnley one, containing Adamson, Elder, McIlroy, Robson and Pointer, which flowered under Harry Potts into the marvellous blend of 1959–1962. What he will never build is a team which believes that nothing at all can come before winning. He sees football as a professional, without a doubt, but he looks to it for uplift before cash. 'Look at the tactical side of it,' he says. 'Look at the joy of a group of men pitting their wits against another. Nothing is more calculated to make a man of you than to run the risk of professional football.'

Brown was born in Consett, Co. Durham. His father was a painter and decorator, and the boy was at grammar school in the late twenties and early thirties. He was an outstanding athlete and he wanted to be a schoolteacher and a professional footballer. Hexham Grammar School played rugby, so he played standoff-half for the school on Saturday mornings and football for a youth side in the afternoons. Being one of four children during the Depression ruled out university. His cousin, then captain of Huddersfield Town, took him into professional football at 16.

Talking 37 years later about his experience on Huddersfield's ground staff Brown remembered a situation very different from that which nurtures young players nowadays. He found the most effective way of getting any attention from the training staff was to block up the fuel jet on the grass cutter. He shook his head: 'I was indeed neglected.' He had hoped to be able to continue studying while with Huddersfield, and in the disappointment of finding no interest in his education he left football and spent two and a half years in the local police force.

The police taught him, although incidentally, how to dig ditches, and he likes to make the point that he is as skilled at the job as any Irish navvy. 'I was digging for days on end,' he said. 'I was keeping observations in a disorderly house case.' The lesson proved valuable to him when he joined Burnley years later as manager. He established the club's spacious outdoor training centre on the outskirts of the town, and he emphasizes now that it was 'literally dug out of the ground' and not only by hired labour. 'The players got down to it – famous ones, like McIlroy and Adamson – and dug ditches with me. And remember this was at the time when professional footballers were supposed to be the most grasping people in the world.'

He had gone back to football because its compulsion was undeniable. He had to return to Huddersfield Town because the rules of the sport at the time did not allow him to change clubs. But after the war Huddersfield transferred him to Burnley, then in Division Two, and in the following season Burnley won promotion and were beaten by 1–0 in the Cup Final. He played briefly later for Notts County, then retired to go back to Burnley and open a restaurant.

His playing career had contained its moments of triumph, but overall it must have been naggingly unsatisfying for a man so engaged by football. He returned to the game a second time because Stanley Rous, then Secretary of the FA, wrote to him to say he was sorry to see him out of football and suggesting points at which he might re-enter it. He applied to Sheffield Wednesday for a job, and spent four seasons with the club as trainer-coach. 'I was happy to be a teacher,' he said. 'I hadn't any thought of being anything else until Burnley invited me to be their manager.'

Burnley, isolated but attractively so in the Lancashire mill and moor country, have always had to apply themselves totally to the playing of the game, because their small resources have never allowed them to attract with trappings. They have stayed since the forties alongside the rich clubs in the League because they have an eye for the very young player of great potential and have built a reputation for knowing how to develop him. The choice of Brown was entirely in character: an ever-busy, engrossed housemaster, to chivvy and coax and command. The business of the ditch-digging confirmed the point. There was nothing aloof or over-theorizing about Brown; he led from among the players, not from his office.

His departure, after three years, to Sunderland had a touch of the crusader's mission about it. He said: 'I was on holiday in Cornwall, away from telephones, and I didn't know there was a story in all the papers saying I was going to take over the Sunderland job. When my secretary at Burnley told me about it I laughed my socks off. But the idea grew on me, being a North-Easterner. I thought I might be able to clean it up. No one else seemed to want the job.' He took Sunderland from the lower reaches of Division Two back into Division One.

Brown's reputation as a trouble-shooter, a man to reclaim and renourish a debilitated club, was established. But the job he now took at Sheffield Wednesday was of a different kind. The club had launched on an ambitious, imaginative rebuilding plan, giving it one of the handsomest settings for football in the League. Brown's concern was to be solely with the team, to try to bring playing success which would give meaning to the management's architectural enterprise. He failed narrowly to win the Cup in 1966; in the early part of the 1967–8 season he had his team briefly at the top of Division One. This was limited success; enough to create bearable tension, to deepen pain in defeat and pleasure in victory to a point well below the skin. He was in the vulnerable position of being a leading manager. Late in the 1967–8 season he returned to Sunderland on a long-term contract.

The weakness of Brown's team at Sheffield, both as a competitor and as an entertainment, was that it lacked any one point of special impact. It was intensely industrious, technically capable and only the unusually strong teams or the unusually gifted could beat it with any effort to spare. It was the sort of side which appeals consistently to supporters without ever scraping their nerve-ends. It usually did incisive and resolute things that spectators could admire; it seldom struck the sparks that dazzle, either individually or collectively.

This, of course, is a spectator's comment. Brown sees football differently. He said to me: 'People complain there's a shortage of *characters* in football nowadays. But when they say that they usually mean *bad* characters.' He shares with Stan Cullis the honest craftsman's view of football: attention to detail, application above all. 'I get an hour's work out of an hour's time,' he said. 'I think I'm known for that.'

At the time I was talking to him he had thirty-three fulltime professionals and fourteen apprentice players at Sheffield. All the formal training was done in the afternoons, although at least half of the players were usually at the ground in the mornings, concentrating on particular aspects of their play; he used the mornings for interviewing parents, checking on injuries, dealing with letters, answering reporters' questions. His relationship with the players, as a group as young as any in the League, involved a brisk, affable authority on his part and a deferential informality on theirs. He said: 'I believe I have to inculcate absolute trust, and that applies even to triviality. I allow myself to be involved when someone comes along with some problem, however small it sounds. If people unload to me I feel stronger after it. If someone believes you're strong, you're half-way there.' The affair of the Cup tickets was an example of 'a group of lads testing the boss', he said, and it was the kind of test a manager could not afford to fail.

An approach to life like this is bound to engender its eccentricities in the running of a football team. Brown has never heard of the permissive society, or if he has he has opted out of it. His creed for footballers' personal conduct is startling. He said: 'I tell all my lads under 21 that they must never let me see them with a cigarette. With those over 21 I advise against it. I advise against drink as well. When we're in public as a club you'll never see a drink. Suppose a man's sitting in a railway carriage with a glass of beer in front of him. Little boys may see it and think it's the right thing to do. If adults see it they put two and two together and make five. I make sure I never have to send for a man for boozing.' He paused, then said: 'I ask – no, I demand – the highest code of conduct.'

It clearly mattered greatly to him to be able to report that his players did not resist this approach. He felt he had established a standard of self-discipline among them which made frequent instruction unnecessary. He said: 'Look, if I'm not back here at two o'clock this afternoon I guarantee that within five minutes the training session would begin, it would go on longer than the one I would give them, and it would be purposeful. That's one of the most rare things in football.' When he was on tour with his team, he said, he could guarantee that if he put his suitcase down on a railway platform the players would immediately line up behind him. 'It's almost military,' he said. 'We don't want some old lady falling over because we've got our bags scattered all over the place.' In Hong Kong he was asked if four of the players could go into the local schools and do some coaching. 'I said, "No, you can have all seventeen, and myself."'

Brown does not make jokes about football. He calls it 'one of the biggest things that's happened in creation – bigger than any "ism" you can name'. For that reason he sees deep significance in the way English footballers conduct thmselves. It goes without need of explanation that such an attitude despises the flamboyance of elaborate hair and sulky ill-temper. The word 'manly' recurs in his conversation.

At 53 Brown was still, by his own definition, 'a tracksuit manager', although his absorption in the game had led him to thoughtful reappraisal of its organization. But he was resigned, he said, to accepting that managers' ideas were largely discounted by authority in football. I quoted him earlier as saying that managers were generally held 'in the contempt we deserve'. He added to this with: 'I say "deserve" because it's no use blaming everyone else in sight. It must be our own fault. We are sacked and kicked around; so many of us work without contracts.' Why was there no effective professional body looking after managers' interests? 'You could say it's expediency, or you might say it's through lack of courage.'

In practice, Brown said, the only way a manager could influence the organization of football was through his directors. And then: 'If you put forward ideas they may be taken up or they may reach fulfilment years afterwards, when they get presented as someone else's work. We're simply not held in very high esteem. All we can achieve is an undercurrent effect.'

This unusual man, impelled by a declared moral passion, has made contributions to football. He sounded most satisfied when he was talking about the success of men he had trained and encouraged when they were young. This is the born teacher's sense of duty, and also his unconscious arrogance. He listed the players who, persuaded into coaching courses by him and helped by his own instruction, had become managers and club coaches. 'I instilled a desire to teach the game,' he said, stressing the verbs with a considerable weight.

Brown plainly recognizes his position of isolation as a manager. It is not enough for him merely to be respected; his team must win more often than it loses. Yet he is not talking about match results when he says: 'It is important to me that I am considered absolutely trustworthy.' Managers make their own decisions about where their responsibility is ultimately owed. With some it is to success; with Brown it is to himself.

3 Stanley Mortensen (and civic pride)

There is an air of good living about Stanley Mortensen, not the abandoned kind which distorts the flesh but the modest, well-ordered sort which comes to the successful and the companionable. There is no introspection in Mortensen's face. The years of intense physical effort are masked by a plump jauntiness. He looks now, in his late 40s, like an enterprising businessman, with strictly local ambitions, who made his mark early and decided he deserved a lifebelt round his waist.

He has, in fact, done well in business, beginning with a postcard shop on Blackpool's Golden Mile of fortune-tellers and candy-floss stalls, and moving on to a sports shop and two betting shops. He adopted Blackpool as his home, just as numerous showbiz people have, attracted and retained by its gregarious bravura. He can hold his corner fluently in the wisecracking rough-and-tumble which is one of the characteristics of the town; there is not much righteousness in the air when Morty is addressing Rotary or the Round Table. He has been an important figure in Blackpool for more than twenty years, as a star footballer, as a town councillor in charge of publicity, and now as manager of the club he played for. Before he took his present job he turned down several offers to manage other clubs. He said to me: 'The thought of leaving Blackpool put me off.'

For that reason Mortensen is one of the least experienced managers in the League. He took over Blackpool in February 1967 just as the club was sliding out of Division One and showing all the signs of a disintegration of the nerve; poor results and dispiritedness breed from each other in sport.

Mortensen seemed well aware, when I talked to him eight months later, that his recuperative effect as a person was more important to his appointment than any tactical insight he could bring to the club. 'The true professional hates to get beat,' he said to me. 'We've got a lot of them here. If you don't get their spirit up you'll never get through to them.' At that time Blackpool were at the top of Division Two. The human tonic bottle, the iron content sweetly concealed to make it more palatable to the patient, was having its bracing effect.

Mortensen was born on Tyneside, his childhood circumstances the archetypal ones for producing urgent footballers of his generation: a poor home surrounded by more. He was 16 when he was taken on by the Blackpool club, but he had not reached the first team by the time he joined the RAF during the war. His progress as a player began with an association with Bath City, never one of the most resounding names in football, and he has always been publicly grateful to that club for giving him a chance to develop competitively. Once his game began to flow he was used by half a dozen of the leading clubs on the wartime 'guest player' basis. Then the Wellington bomber he was in caught fire and crashed, and Mortensen was carried away from the wreckage with a deep gash along the base of his skull.

He was told not to expect to play football again; but he played twenty-five times for England, and collected a Cup winners' medal. The crash left him with insomnia, which he has lived with ever since, and a scar which supports his assertion that he is one of the luckiest men alive. It is a curved line across the back of his neck, on a level with the top of his ear lobes and a good four inches long. He keeps his hair long enough at the back to cover it, but will show it on request, bending his head low and palming his back hair up. 'Eh?' he says, and looks up at the ceiling, astonished still.

Mortensen was very much a star of his period, associated in our minds mostly as the inside-right or centre-forward to Matthews's right-wing play: a decisive goalscorer, not equipped for any intricate use of the ball but swift and clean-cut when he was going forward with it. He was one of the players who brought the setpiece style to its peak, he being the darting loose forward, overlooked by the opposition as it was drawn to the dribbler with the ball, who would materialize suddenly to seize on the final pass. But because he was essentially an opportunist, concerned with stealing away from a defence when he did not have the ball, he was nearer to today's forwards than were most of his contemporaries. To use the jargon of the sixties, he was good 'off the ball'. He would cover perhaps 40 yards in a run to meet the final pass close to goal, the improvised movement just as deadly as some of the pre-packed ones by which modern inside forwards arrive in the goal area from the half-way line to score with their only kick at the ball in a rehearsed attack. It is for this reason that the modern game does not appear to him to be as different from that of the forties as some would say it is.

Nor did Mortensen disappear quickly from the game when he found he was no longer fast enough for Division One. He went from Blackpool to Hull, then to Southport. When he was seriously considering retiring for good he was given an opportunity to repay the debt he always felt he owed to Bath City. He said: 'The chairman of Bath came to Blackpool for a holiday, and he said to me, "Well, you look fit enough, so why don't you come and play for us for a season?"' So Mortensen graced the Southern League for a while, making the long drive down every Saturday morning and reversing it after the match. When this began to tell on him he let himself be persuaded to play for Lancaster City in the Lancashire Combination for a year.

By now he was over 40, and he was already more of a practical demonstrator for the younger players around him than an imposing performer. 'I thought I was doing a worthwhile job,' he said. 'I was passing on knowledge, you see.' He was reluctant to leave the game, still excited by it even at this level, which was pedestrian in comparison with what he had once known. Its pull was in its appeal to the nervous system; he was not merely trying to keep the years off his back. He said: 'There's that moment when you run on to the pitch. It's always been the same, whatever class of football I was in. I always got butterflies before every game. It never made any difference whether I was playing for England, Blackpool or Lancaster. There was something in that moment like nothing else. I had to keep playing as long as I possibly could.' Even in 1967, aged 46, he was playing charity matches in a team of veterans called Stanley Mortensen's International XI. I was not allowed to get away with a smile at that. 'It's a good class of football,' he said, entirely serious.

I was talking to one of the definitive figures of his generation, rather rolled in shape now in his shortie overcoat, the hair greased flat and parted in a white cleft, the words 'local pride' and 'local loyalty' on his lips like parts of a litany. He saw duty in his job, a responsibility to football as a whole as well as an overriding one to his town. He said he was certain that an appeal to footballers' sense of local responsibility could increase their resolve. He said: 'When I send my men out on to the field I say to them in so many words, "Don't forget that jersey you're wearing represents the people of Blackpool".' This is the commitment of a man who will never see the game principally as an entertainment industry. He was first conditioned to it when it was an habitual release from an everyday world which was generally unpromising, to say the most for it. Unlike today's star players, who have a readier mobility, socially and professionally, Mortensen always felt himself a part of the community that watched him play, not just an idol of it. He was playing on his neighbours' behalf.

He said that as a manager he was anxious to foster much more local involvement by his players. The more highly they regarded the town the more effort they would put into their work, he thought; and the supporters' criticism would be better informed, if only by sympathy. He said: 'I've always felt that footballers ought to involve themselves more than they do. It's a duty really, and it helps them put across how they feel about things.'

This is the opposite of an objective view of football. It reflects a deep fondness for the sport of a kind which, in a thinner personality, might be distinct solemnity; but it is certainly an insider's view. Mortensen was looking for goals to come out of insistence before anything else. Any amateurs' team captain would recognize this rallying cry. Mortensen represents the sport content in football, even though it is the uncompromising kind, rather than the commercial enterprise in it.

Yet he was clearly well aware of the extensive encroachment of economics on his game. Considering the Saturday atmosphere of the forties and fifties with the one he knows now, he said: 'Oh yes, it's a lot harder commercially.' It meant that no manager seriously looking for success could afford to let his preferences for certain types of player blind him to the greater effectiveness of others, less attractive. It meant that skilful players were undoubtedly being left out of teams because there were cruder ones who would follow instructions more closely and not endanger the structure of a tight defensive method. He said: 'Managers just can't take the risks that a lot of them would like to take. That includes me.'

But Mortensen sees much in the modern game that elates him. He particularly enjoys the marked improvement in the players' fitness, in the greater overall pace of the game, and in the readier adaptability of players between one skill and another. More imaginative and far more professional training had led to these advances, he said. 'With the variety of training nowadays these lads just don't know how hard they're working. With us it used to be, "Get out on the park and keep running".'

The passage of time will establish whether a generous-spirited, civic-minded optimist like Mortensen can retain these qualities as a football manager and achieve continuing success. The strength of his will is not in dispute; what will be tested is its nature.

4 Sir Matt Busby (and virtuosity)

To watch Sir Matt Busby move about Manchester is to observe a public veneration. He is not merely popular; not merely respected for his flair as a manager. People treat Busby in the way that middle-aged priests of compassionate and sporty nature are often treated: the affection becomes rapidly more deferential as they get nearer to the man. Small boys rush noisily towards him, holding their picture books out for his autograph, and fall silent and shy once they get up close and he calls for less jostling and settles the word 'son' upon them like a blessing. Adults shout his first name and grab for his hand. They wave at him in his car. When he was made a Freeman of Manchester in 1967 there was a marked sense of public approval for authority: the Town Hall had done something right for a change. Whatever was involved in being a Freeman it sounded the sort of title Matt ought to have before anybody else. Would there be a statue?

Busby had made Manchester United the most successful English football club since the war: FA Cup winners in 1948 and 1963, losers in the Final in 1957 and 1958; League champions in 1952, 1956, 1957, 1965 and 1967, and six times runners-up; winners of the European Cup at the close of the 1967–8 season (soon after which Busby was knighted). In imposing his personality overwhelmingly on his club he has won a rare place as the city's constant hero, outlasting the players, growing old with the fans. The special emotional attachment which the Munich disaster established between people and club applies specifically to him, because he was desperately injured and yet survived. He has had an extraordinary life, and its explosive drama has not disrupted his dignity as a man nor his vision as a manager.

Busby is not far off 60 now. He runs his club from one of the most elegant offices in the Football League, a sanctum for a calm executive, furnished and carpeted with an eye to comfort. It is not protected from reporters with anything approaching the obstructions to be found in front of several less successful managers, who treat questions with more suspicion than confidence. But he is not an easy-going man. He likes to answer carefully and without ambiguity, and visitors are not allowed to hear his part of the dialogue in intervening telephone conversations. 'If you don't mind, please?,' he will say, pointing his pipe at the door, 'it's private.' He gives an impression of great power of concentration, and as with men of such capacity in other fields he can apply himself totally to an entertaining geniality when he decides to switch off from work. His tension shows in his urgent movements and the impatience for the bone of the matter when the questions turn speculative and flabby. He treats journalists as if they are part of his own world, and again it is an attitude he shares with other successful men, particularly politicians. His success as a manager lies principally in his almost impeccable judgement of a player; his place in public esteem has been secured by his substance as a person.

In the twenty-two seasons Busby has had at Old Trafford he has earned the club an aggregate cash profit of well over £500,000. The difference between what he has spent on his current League team and what it would fetch on the transfer market must be approaching another half-million pounds. In terms of business acumen alone he is entirely suited to his well-cut clothes and the heavy Rover with its leather interior. The rich presence is proper to a man paying out wages to Jag drivers.

His relationship with his players is a special combination of the austere and the engrossed. He is a family-man Catholic, and in his control of the club there is a lot of the character of a stern, devoted grandfather, making all the big decisions, ordering and disciplining in some huge, unpredictably gifted household. I am not the only writer to have described Busby as a patriarch; his manner and his method attract the word.

I asked him if his players were shy of him, and he said he found the younger ones often nervous and speechless when they first joined the club. 'I encourage them to be natural with me,' he said, and it was the comment of a man whose success depends on his bridging a wide gulf between generations. When he arrives in the middle of a training session there is an immediate subduing of noise and a sense of heightened activity. He likes to interfere as little as possible with his players' lives away from the club, but when they are at work he is totally in charge. 'I'll just have a word with these boys,' he says quietly, and when he walks out of the training hall the team follows him instantly.

Like many of the best managers Busby was a halfback. He played with Liverpool and Manchester City, and he captained Scotland at wing-half. When he took over Manchester United in 1945 the club had been physically wrecked by the war: no stand, no dressing-rooms; matches had to be played on City's ground. In a sense this situation helped him. It gave Old Trafford an overall atmosphere of a brand new beginning. Busby knew exactly what kind of club he wanted, and there was little of what remained of the old one to distract him from his purpose.

He said: 'I always wanted – let me get the right word for it – creative football. I wanted method. I wanted to manage the team as I felt players wanted to be managed. To begin with I wanted a more humane approach than there was when I was playing. Sometimes lads were just left on their own. The first team hardly recognized the lads underneath. There never seemed to be enough interest taken in players. The manager was at his desk, and you saw him once a week. From the start I tried to make the smallest member think he was part of the club.'

Busby did not invent the youth policy in football which has been so important in the development of the game since the war; but more than any other manager he put his faith and his reputation into it. He had a clear mental picture of the kind of football he wanted, and he created a side to match it. This was the brilliantly gifted, but intensely methodical, team of the fifties, different from any other in that it was almost wholly composed of young, home-trained players. Its only spectacular purchase from outside was its centre-forward, Tommy Taylor, who came from Barnsley for the memorable sum of £29,999. The lounge at Old Trafford has among its trophies a plaque which marks the winning of the FA Youth Cup in three successive seasons, 1953–4–5, and it represents Busby's imaginative work as much as does his success in the senior competitions. The three seasons proved his method and made the later triumphs possible.

The Munich crash destroyed the side of the fifties, preventing us from ever knowing how great it could be in full maturity; it had perhaps two more years to reach its peak. Busby's severe injuries, the immediate need to gather another side together and the continuing necessity for strong reinforcement as the competition gained momentum made it impossible for the club to revert fully to Busby's original method. United's teams since Munich have never lacked brilliance, but the word 'methodical' has had much less relevance. There is poignancy in the fact that the most innovating mind in post-war British football was allowed briefly to see his creation acclaimed but had to accept that there could be no resurrection. There would be more success, but it would come in a different way.

Busby still adds persistently to his string of precocious, home-bred youngsters, who spring highly gifted and astonishingly assured out of the nursery and into the adult conflict without a falter. Best was acquired, like Charlton and his pre-Munich friends before, immediately out of school; Stiles was home-produced, and so were Kidd and Burns, the new names of 1967. But Busby has also bought, certainly expensively but with great discrimination. Law came back from Italy, in a confusion of competitive bartering, at a price of £115,000; Pat Crerand cost £50,000, Alex Stepney £60,000; Albert Quixall, David Herd and John Connelly all cost major sums and were bought, and used, for specialized jobs. But the turnover in players has always been small; a manager who sees clearly what kind of football he wants regards his time wasted if he has to spend much of it as a dealer.

Consistently over the years Busby has put together teams which dazzle. Since Munich he has settled for virtuosity. Only the Tottenham team which won the Cup and the League championship in 1961, then the Cup again the following year, has been able to match the inborn flair of the side containing Best, Charlton, Crerand and Law. Its inconsistency through the seasons, often scrambling draws when the gap in talent between the two sides ought to have given it clear victory, comes from this very inspirational content: the temperamental tautness which goes with it prevents reliability. Sometimes the defence, always second string to the attack, has summoned an organic resolution beyond its normal capacity; usually the forwards must take control of the game on behalf of the team. When they do it with the full flow of their talents they produce football of an elegance and an explosiveness which make it incomparable sport.

Busby's team has drawn huge crowds all over the country

E

for the prospect of what it may do this time, not on the basis of how it was last time out.

Busby believes in a long, loose rein for his star players once they are on the field. In his earlier years as a manager he spent most of the day in his tracksuit. Now he puts it on once or twice a week, more to sustain the communication between himself and the players than to demonstrate what he wants from them. He says: 'I like to get in among them a bit. I doddle round with them.' When I talked to him just before he became a Freeman of Manchester he said it was nine months since he last gave one of his little lectures on tactics at the blackboard. He regarded organization of the side not as the crux of its performance, as it is with some other leading clubs, but as an overall understanding of individual roles. 'The team needs to know what is expected of one another,' he said. 'I don't want to take players off their game.' A bad performance, though, was always followed by one of his quiet, intense talks, with detailed instructions, whose objects were 'to get them back to where they were'.

He agrees that he has to treat his forwards and his defenders differently, although his public loyalty to his players does not permit him to accept that the gulf in talent which other people see actually exists. Certainly the forwards have brilliance, he says; and certainly they have glamour; but the defenders 'know their jobs, even if they are not lauded as much'. But he concedes that defensive play is 'more teachable' than the attacking kind; defenders can be taught a great deal about positioning, tackling and 'keeping in touch with each other', whereas the abilities of Best and Charlton are special to them.

Busby makes sure that he sees as much as time allows of his reserve and junior players, his eye still restless for the boy of brilliant promise. I asked him if he thought it was possible for the able manager to miss the qualities of an outstanding young player. He said: 'I don't think it is. He may have a bad game the day you watch him, but there will be something about him that strikes you. There's something in the really gifted player that hits you. Is "instinct" the right word? You look for that.'

There is coolness in Busby's view of football; it is the deliberate consideration of a man who lives by it and must retain his judgement at all costs. His involvement is total, but he seems consciously to subdue his passion for the game. Stan Cullis says that he once told Busby how much he envied his calm during a match; Busby told him he should not be deceived by appearances.

The process which results in a leading manager's decision to secure a promising young player in the face of other clubs' competition is complex, as I tried to show in the first chapter. Busby is helped in it by a training staff, headed by his assistant for many years, Jimmy Murphy (the club's caretaker manager while Busby was recovering from the air crash), and by Joe Armstrong's scouting staff. For every Charlton, Best and Burns, there are a score of boys who have much of the skill but not enough of the vital quality which tells. Is it definable? Busby said: 'You can only call it temperament in the end. I've seen so many lads who look outstanding players in the reserves, but just can't make it in the first team. That's the big question. There's something special in the atmosphere in the first team, and I've seen many good, clever players who just can't catch it. It's not fair to call it courage.'

Letters from hopeful young players, and from parents, teachers and fans, arrive by the hundred at Old Trafford every year, recommending talent. The screening system is careful; there is deep anxiety that great potential should not slip through the net. Some of the credit for United's eye for young promise and capacity for development must go to Busby's staff; but in the end the decision, along with the congratulations and the blame, must be with the manager. Busby's record in the acquisition of players of the highest ability, often while they have been still at school, has not been matched by any other British manager in the last twenty years. On this talent he has largely built his success, and because of it his has been one of the paramount individual contributions to the game.

It has been complained against Busby that for so important a figure in the sport he permits too much petulance by some of his players, too much flaunting of personality both on the field and off it. Perhaps the team he created in the fifties, linked so closely to his own character, would have been less offensive in this way; perhaps a man who has seen so much exuberance crushed in a single, frightful moment cannot be expected to be harsh with it when it appears, even if more showily, in a later generation.

5 Sir Alf Ramsey (and strategy)

In football, as in any sport, victory and defeat are repeatedly decided on the knife-edge of chance. Sir Alf Ramsey, manager of the England team since 1962, has applied himself more than anyone else in the game to blunting that murderous edge. Ramsey's job is very different from that of a club manager, who puts a team together for long-term success and can concentrate his money and his faith in certain departments of his side, relying on the day-to-day contact of the players to sustain the dovetailing understanding any side needs. Ramsey has his players under his instruction only occasionally, and then briefly; so he has sought a team whose individual talents and personalities would cohere because of their nature, since time is such a frail ally. His first duty is to help England win the World Cup, he says; he succeeded in 1966 with a climactic final at Wembley stadium whose emotional tension brought even mature and discreetly dressed people to tears.

That match, in which England beat West Germany 4–2, was a constant crescendo of drama. England were leading 2–1 in the last minute of the normal ninety; fifteen seconds from the end the Germans equalized after a free kick dubiously awarded against Jack Charlton. The England players wrung our hearts with their exhaustion and dejection, as the two teams sank to the grass for the short interval before the half-hour of extra time, and the picture of Ramsey, stocky and grave, walking towards them without a suggestion of haste was unforgettable; he braced the spectators as well as the players. England outpaced the opposition comprehensively when the game restarted, and their last goal was Geoff Hurst's marvellous shot into the roof of the net after a run of thirty yards in the final minute. In the delirious jubilation which followed, with players leaping about, lifting each other in the air, and some of them sobbing, Ramsey was still sedate, his smile the thinnest of slits between his lips. He moved abruptly only to stop the England players from exchanging shirts with their opponents. He had to be physically dragged by the players into the groups the photographers were trying to assemble. At last he allowed himself to be persuaded into what he clearly regarded as an excessively flamboyant gesture; he kissed the cup.

This public impassivity becomes a terse, contemplative wariness in private. Ramsey is not a popular man, either with other professionals in the game or with journalists, in the superficial sense of affable familiarity. His private personality, of course, could not possibly be the almost haughtily detached one which he offers to the world a very long arm's length away; his public composure is an obsessive self-defence. But people who know him well – or, at least, see him frequently, which would be the same thing with most other men – have lots of stories to illustrate his incommunicability and none which have him telling jokes over large dollops of the hard stuff. His cold dignity is certainly not an act. As with brilliant players his approach to football comes from deep inside the man. The performances of his team in 1966 reflected his character truthfully.

Some of the language in which Ramsey's management has been discussed has confused the issue greatly. People talked and wrote of him 'gambling' on a side without specialist wingers, on Roger Hunt's pedestrian honesty of effort, on Bobby Moore's ability to lift his play for the biggest occasions. The essence of Ramsey's handling of the England team has been exactly the opposite of the gambler's manner. He aimed at removing risk. Considering my opening sentence in this character study it might appear that such an approach must inevitably be self-defeating; but Ramsey's job is special in that he cannot budget for the occasional defeat in a long struggle for eventual triumph. In the World Cup matches, which are his prime responsibility, he must not lose.

It is extraordinary to reflect on how insular the British attitude to football was even as recently as the early sixties. Reference to 4–2–4 or 4–3–3 formations were then being dismissed by many observers as pretentious jargon-dropping, or were laughed off as 'the numbers game'. Ramsey was asked incredulously in print whether he seriously intended to put out an international side without recognized wingers. The snappy question on the sports pages was: What's it all about, Alf?

What it was all about was that England's place in world

football was being considered for the first time by a strategist with no past decisions to defend, total personal responsibility and an awareness that the nature of the opposition was crucially important to the composition of his own team. He took an open mind to the England team; a stone cold one, in fact. He applied the principles already being used by club managers: that success was overridingly important, that positive method was indispensable, that attractiveness was incidental. He did not give players positional titles; he gave them jobs. He had in his mind a picture of a team in movement, not of names on a sheet of paper.

The word Ramsey has used in retrospect, when talking about his team, is 'blend'. He is not an easy man to quote, partly because he objects to discussing individual players for the public ear, and secondly because he is simply a poor talker. Many a sympathetically interpretive interview with Ramsey has been lost to the public because his self-conscious concern with his vowels and his aspirates can diminish his words to close on worthlessness. When frustrated reporters have wanted to be posh about him they have tended to call him 'impenetrable'. He is more literally tongue-tied, although not with his players, of course, since he assumes in them a knowledge of his professionals' language. He is the antithesis of Busby, in his confrontation with the public, in that he appears to believe that if he opens up his mind to them they will not understand a word he is talking about. This may be nothing more than total, professional absorption with the game. Among all the people who wrote reams about the World Cup for money Ramsey was the most conspicuous absentee.

Ramsey's objective rapport with the game developed alongside his intent application to it. The grocer's boy from Dagenham played for Southampton, then for Tottenham and made over thirty appearances for England at right-back: a studious, undemonstrative, uncompromising defender. He retired from playing at 35 and became manager of Ipswich, and his performance in taking them from the middle of the Second Division to the very top of the First was a telling indication of his managerial insight. Week by week in the seasons 1960–62 other teams' supporters watched the canny, lack-lustre Ipswich stun more glamorous sides with a crushing, overall solidity of method. There were two big strikers up at the front to bang in the goals, never prettily, and behind them the machine pounded diligently and expertly. Perhaps there has never been a duller championship side, and its success was the more commendable for that. Footballers can be berated for not being highly talented, but it is no use blaming them for winning.

This experience with Ipswich confirmed Ramsey in the lesson he was to apply to his job as England's manager. Individual ability was relevant only when it connected collectively. It is irrelevant to complain that Ramsey ignores flair in preference for physical strength and work-rate; what he looks for is maximum effectiveness from eleven players. This does not exclude specialists of the highest quality, as was shown in Hurst's hat-trick in the World Cup Final. But it does exclude the virtuoso limited by, and to, his one high talent. What I understood Ramsey to be telling me, when I talked to him in the seemly comfort of the FA's reception room in Lancaster Gate, was that he rejected conventional wingers for the World Cup because the opposition was too strong to be dominated by any one such specialist available to him. That deficiency did not just rule out certain individuals; it ruled out their kind, not for good but for the particular job in hand.

By the same token there were certain players he clearly regarded as central to his purpose, because talent and character fused in them: Stiles, Moore, Ball, Hunt. Banks was in goal on the basis of being the best man at that particular job in Britain, and probably in the world; neither of the Charlton brothers had serious opposition for places, nor did Cohen and Wilson; Peters and Hurst won places as specialists, Peters being the best available football version of the rugby scrum-half, at once reliable and inspirational, Hurst being the front striker. Critics argued at the time of the World Cup Final, and argue still, on behalf of claimants for at least two of these places. Ramsey's point was entirely proved: he got the blend, and he got the results.

Ramsey's confidences are so rare that they crackle in the air. He said to me: 'I tried nine centre-forwards in three years; but I knew months, even years, before the World Cup that Bobby Charlton would have a number nine on his back.' This was intriguing, and illuminating, because it destroyed certain popular beliefs about Ramsey's blind attachment to other, very different kinds of players. Again the point was that where the special talents were high enough they chose themselves; not because they happened to fit but because they helped to decide the fit. I pursued the point by asking Ramsey if this meant that had Charlton suddenly gone down with 'flu, or had broken a leg, would he have looked round for another exponent of the style, and he said sharply: 'No, there wasn't one.' In other words the make-up and method of the England team could have been substantially different without Charlton.

So how much for Ramsey's reliance on controlled method, given the well-known changeability in Charlton's form? Well, football is not mathematics. No manager can eliminate chance; he can only protect himself against its ill effects to his utmost ability. 'You can't budget entirely for the Bobby Charltons and the Martin Peters of this world, because of their natural instinct to go forward,' Ramsey says. 'When I am picking my strongest side I pick the players who are strongest in their positions.' He is talking of the positions in his own, special vision of a moving team. Methods, he said, might change. 'But when they do I will know exactly what we are trying to do, and so will the players.'

It is not beyond Ramsey to take an entirely different team and approach to the World Cup in Mexico in 1970 from those which won him his knighthood in 1966. It was his cold, unprejudiced appraisal which produced the right blend for the occasion, and how closely he tries to repeat it will depend on what changes occur in other countries' football as well as on the quality of English players then available to him.

His, as he put it with another of those most unwilling of smiles, is 'a curious job'. He does not live, as club managers do, by the weekly ups and downs of the same dozen men on the plump part of the payroll. He does not watch football with his heart in his mouth, taut with anxiety for goals. He watches individual players, dispassionate for their success or failure, noting their advantages and their weaknesses, his mind endlessly taking in and rejecting new faces in the constant search for 'the blend'. This search takes him all over England, concentrating on the First and Second Divisions but including the Third and Fourth as well.

He said: 'I work to a pattern to allow me to see every First Division player who is eligible to play for England, and as many players in the other divisions as possible. I prefer to arrange it so that I am watching a player away from home.'

He travels abroad a great deal, so that he can see the nature of the coming opposition. It is a distinctly solitary life, and people close to him in the sport say he is growing gradually less approachable. He tries to make sure that he is at home with his wife on Sundays.

He was most relaxed when he was talking about the way the football followers treat him. As he walks from some club car park to the ground people tend to talk loudly about his team, not to his face but in elaborate efforts to make sure he hears them: he ought to try So-and-so; why doesn't this character Ramsey get a decent centre-forward/centre-half/right-back, like yon So-and-so? He smiles at this advice, as he does about the spate of letters which arrives in his office after most international matches. He said: 'They tend to start off with things like, "Dear Stupid" or "Dear Big Head". One man wrote to me, beginning "Dear Alfie Boy". If it's a good match, and it gets a good write-up in the press, there won't be many letters.' Parents write to him urging him to try their sons in the England team; his mail, in fact, is principally loaded with advice on who should be in his side.

Ramsey dresses carefully, and in terms of haircut and collars and cuffs is impeccably groomed. He is plainly deeply conscious of his position – in the responsible sense, not the pompous one. There is as much shyness in the man as self-assurance. He is aware that a great deal of emotional involvement in the country is tied to his judgement as a professional. In spite of his smooth turn-out this weight of responsibility prevents even surface urbanity: the public composure, immensely impressive at a distance, changes into a deliberate self-control which is both less intimidating and more affecting close up.

I asked him if he still enjoyed football as much as he did as a young player, half expecting a defensive prevarication about objectivity, but he smiled in frank surprise at the question and said that he certainly did. The exercise of a dominant will may be no light matter, but it has its depth of pleasure.

3 The Director

The institution of the football club director is the sport's central contradiction. The amateurs govern the professionals. The situation is repeated in the moment of conflict, when a part-time referee can order an international star player off the field, and again in the overall conduct of the sport, which is in the hands of the family doctors, head-teachers and variety of master tradesmen who make up the Council of the FA.

The club director is the person in whom the fanaticism of the terraces and the urge for authority fuse. He is imbued with a desire to manage, yet is activated principally by his partisan local involvement and the moral approach he brings to the wider issue. He is principally a committee man in a business which increasingly needs the incisiveness of the singular will. He is still entirely appropriate to Bath City; in Division One he is either incongruously obtrusive or sensibly passive. Where the competition is toughest the best service he can render his club is to pick the best manager he can find, and afford, and allow him to do his job. Too often he finds such self-effacement too wounding to be sustained. This is not surprising. The football club boardroom is an enviable place to a man committed to his town and to the game, and the delightful condition of smoking a cigar in it is not conducive to modesty.

Being a director does not make money for a man, at any rate not directly, since directors are prohibited from receiving salaries. Most directors are businessmen, not executives of large, compartmental corporations but heads of local firms, because local commitment goes with immobility; so the status of the directorship is considerable, and one of the most unequivocal of club chairmen told me firmly that 'being a director brings in business'. But that is a variable asset, depending on the business the man is in, the success of the team and the size of the town. A National Health doctor cannot be much helped by it; a meat-pie maker or central heating engineer may well be. But the FA limits the dividend a club may pay its shareholders to 7·5 per cent gross, which makes any direct profit minimal. In any case some clubs' trading results, year by year, are as often losses as gains, and even with the most successful clubs money is only relevant in terms of the football it can give its supporters. If professional football were to be run as a thoroughgoing business enterprise the fans would hardly be placated in their disappointment at failure by the knowledge that the shareholders had had a good year.

Football grounds are not often attractive places in the ornamental sense. Their beauty is the special, environmental kind, appreciable only to people who relate the setting to their emotional attachment. Football's history decreed that the grounds should be cavernous and stark: sport's version of the gloomy, comfortless factories for whose workers they were built. Most are little different today from when they were established in the first quarter of the century, and they are monuments to the general poverty of the period and the absence of aesthetic consideration which went with it. Where the supporters' concern is deepest and the goals most fiercely contested, thousands still stand on greasy steps, trapped for a couple of hours in a swaying crush of bodies, frequently forced off their feet in a delirious surge of mass movement, and they come away with bruises and the stains of other people's shoes. The director probably first knew his football in this damp, eruptive, acrid confusion.

By the time he reaches the boardroom, with its mahogany smelling of furniture polish and the titans of long ago frowning down from their sombre picture-frames wearing singing-waiter moustaches and high boots, he has graduated from the terraces and the rudimentary bench seating and then the tip-up kind which goes with the more expensive season tickets. He has acquired his shares in the club through some relative, perhaps distant, or from a well-connected friend. He is voted a director because his devotion to the club has been proved by the years, or because he has established his support for a demand for new staff, or because he is openly ambitious for the eventual chairmanship and has lobbied diligently, even ruthlessly, to corner voting shares and lieutenants. Once arrived he will fight hard to keep his place; and only a collective catastrophe, such as a dramatic slide into ignominy by the team, may shift him while his health lasts.

Some degree of wealth is essential to the completion of this process. Not only is it the accepted proof of identity in the local Establishment but sometimes directors are expected to guarantee a sum of money should the club need to muster some last-ditch resources to pay bills: £2,000 is perhaps an average figure per man under these circumstances, although the director's guarantee is a less common feature than it used to be now that the economics of football are on a higher level, both in substance and sophistication. Supporters' clubs nowadays put more money into football than boards of directors do.

Among the better organized clubs, whose boards are composed in an atmosphere of objective selection rather than factious intrigue, directors may have special duties, as in the case of those in large industries. One man will be in charge of catering, another concerned with the condition of the premises, another with training equipment. For this reason the directors will be specialists in their own right, and on the board for that reason. Clubs like these try to ensure that they do not assemble a board which wants to be a team selection committee, which is how the least useful ones behave.

Directors under the age of 45 are not common, and those under 40 distinctly rare. There is an immediate similarity in age group, worldly experience and physical look between football directors and magistrates' benches or municipal watch committees: feet-on-the-ground citizenry, local boys made good none too early in life, no fancy talk, a bit booze-stained round the edges, a high incidence of waistcoats.

This narrow grouping is inevitable, given the setting of football. Since directors may not be paid, by FA rule, few men can find the time to join a board while they are still building their businesses or establishing their careers. Because of the limitations on the influence any other director but the chairman can have on a club's management only the patient or the blatantly ambitious will join in the first place. Managerial flair pays directors only in terms of a boost to the ego or the fan's satisfaction in overtaking the opposition down the road. Such rewards are important in football, but nobody can buy bread with them.

Let me refer to two classic instances of the traditional fan-turned-director: Harold Needler, the chairman of Hull City, and Bob Lord, chairman of Burnley. Personal style separates them widely; their longing for the success of their clubs and the insistence with which they seek it link them almost like spiritual twins.

Needler is an urbane kind of Mr Moneybags, a gently spoken, affable man in company, with a wiry thread of resolution and assurance quickly discernible just below the skin surface. Some men look rich by manner more than trappings and he is one of them: one of the local squires of industry whose sense of security and influence speaks for itself in an unbreachable certainty of a malleable world. Needler virtually owns Hull City.

I met him first in March 1966, on General Election day, which was given an extra electricity in Hull because on that afternoon the place was gathering its strength for an FA Cup sixth round replay with Chelsea in the evening. There had been a time in very recent memory when the turnstiles at Boothferry Park creaked painfully with the stiffness of under-use. But the club was now in the full spate of a zestful revival, and three hours before the kick-off there was a queue of people stretching for half a mile along the avenues of the housing estate which surrounds the ground. The chairman stepped out of his car to a round of applause as seemly as the one which acknowledges the Royal box at Wimbledon. Squirearchy, even the kind that cultivates gravel pits, is treated differently from football professionals.

I talked to him in the referee's room, which seemed to be the only spot in the ground not besieged by ticket hunters. The pleasurable excitement of the day kept a tense smile on his face most of the time we talked. Large amounts of champagne or the sudden news of a massive win on the Pools can settle the same heady geniality on people. This was clearly one of the marvellous days of Harold Needler's life.

Now middle-aged he had been a Hull City supporter since he was among the smaller figures in the boys' enclosure. He could remember that the first match he ever saw was when Hull played Crystal Palace on December 31, 1921. He could improve on this capacity for distant detail by delightedly naming referees in Hull's Cup matches in the thirties. This mass of seemingly trivial information, recalled to mind without recourse to the record books, is the mark of the obsessed football follower. Needler agreed gladly that if he were not rich and the chairman of the club he would certainly have been somewhere in that anxious queue outside the gates.

Money put him into the boardroom. Immediately after the war the club was in a sad and tattered state. Needler had made a fortune in the quarry business, and he bought the ground for £10,500. He has been chairman of the club ever since.

The insular, docks-and-fishing town on the north of the Humber estuary lacks the concentration of heavy industry and urban population which most commonly go with successful football clubs. But in the late forties Hull won their way out of Division Three into Division Two, and stayed there until the mid fifties. By March 1966, with a grey old fox called Cliff Britton as manager, they were about to win promotion into the Second Division again.

Needler had firm views on how this club should be run. He knew, particularly, what kind of manager he needed. He said that his manager 'has got to have the kind of character people can look up to', and he went on: 'He's got to be able to control men, some of whom are very tough. Above all, his players have got to know that he's fair to them.' Looking for long-term success, Needler had given Britton a ten-year contract, an extraordinary incident in British football. To back his man with bedrock resources Needler settled on the club shares in his quarry company worth £200,000 (worth more than twice that by 1966), and he followed up with several substantial private loans.

The money had been spent imaginatively: a strengthening of the playing staff matched by fullscale improvements to the ground, so that when the fans came back to see their side winning again they were not repelled by discomfort. Three new forwards cost £120,000, a new stand £130,000 and floodlighting £50,000. Another £50,000 bought a new gymnasium built to Britton's specification: a specialists' training centre, two-thirds the size of a football pitch, marked out with circles and rectangles for tactical instruction and not cluttered by irrelevant gymnast's equipment such as wallbars, ropes or mats. A few other clubs have training halls of this type, notably Manchester United and Burnley, and most of them are more glamorous names than Hull.

It was Needler's special position as the property owner which allowed him to push this policy through in the face of protracted grumbling by the supporters. Unwilling to watch the team struggle week by week, as the new concrete slowly took shape and the training methods gradually built a new force on the field, the fans stayed away by the drove. The gates sank to as little as 4,000; the town seethed with discontent at 'fancy ideas'. A board of directors with individual influence more evenly shared among the members might well have veered off the policy in panic and gone for quicker, less ambitious success. Needler stuck resolutely to the plan he had agreed with his manager. One hour before the start of the 1966 Cup replay against Chelsea there were 45,000 people in the ground.

Hull lost that match 3–1, Chelsea being a markedly vivacious and inventive side, trimmed to apparent weightlessness by their manager of the period, Tommy Docherty; but Hull went on to win the Division Three championship, four points clear of the runners-up. The Press was most generously treated after the Chelsea game, Mr Needler and his wife taking over the running of the bar when every other club representative had been outlasted.

'Here's to Europe,' the jokers kept saying, between the whisky gulping, the thought of Hull City *v* Real Madrid boggling the leadening mind. Needler's smile glinted right through the night. The Press box had been as packed as the terraces, and that was how he wished it always was.

One of the reasons why Burnley's Press box is often less than packed is the readiness of its chairman to ban reporters from it. Bob Lord, chairman since 1955, has been labelled in print as 'the Khrushchev of Burnley', and insulting as that description was it had a certain physical aptness, bearing in mind Khrushchev's habit of pounding furniture with a heavy right fist. Lord would be equally insulted by any suggestion that he was not firmly in command of the club. His rule has been insistent, and it has been rewarded with success. Since he won the chairmanship he has resoundingly refused to canvass or ingratiate to retain his position. He said to me: 'I say to our directors every year, "Look, if you don't want me again that's all right by me."' But then he added: 'I think those who lifted me out of the chair might find they had a fight on their hands.' He is certainly not a chairman to be shifted by gentle persuasion.

Lord is a passionate partisan of his town and his football team. He is now 60, and he has been running his own businesses since he was 19. He is a florid butcher with a string of shops which he controls from a big office, frequently and tersely on the telephone, not fond of giving the same instructions twice, too decisive and self-convinced to want to waste time arguing about them. Nobody would ever offend him by describing him as self-made or as a typical, old school, Lancashire employer. He said: 'Ask anyone who works for me whether I pay good wages, and they'll tell you, "yes". Then ask them whether I make them work hard, and they'll tell you I'm a slave driver. I don't think I'm that, but I expect something back for my money.'

His busy, impatient manner and the abrasive edge in the voice suggest all the time an embattled man. 'Everything I've ever had in life I've had to fight for,' he said. 'I've got a maxim in life. If ever someone beats me in a battle, I don't blame them. I blame myself for letting them do it. Then I say, "Where have I gone wrong?"' His attitude to football is this same combative, implacable address to a world full of obstructions to be forced aside and snares to be uprooted. But he is an impelled fan of the game, as well. His dedication to becoming master of the club was born of enthralment by football before concern with status.

Lord has never been among the entrenched old guard of club directors, opposed to every change. He was one of the loudest voices in support of the players' demand for higher wages at a time when the League, generally, was reacting like between-the-wars coal owners confronted by hunger marchers. He has berated other League members for their stubborn adherence to ancient methods which, he believes, have strangled development of the game: he has called not only for professional directors but for professional referees as well. If his delivery is often coarse, his unassailable conviction of being right often infuriating, there has often been bold innovation and good sense in his view of football's future.

But Lord does not make friends and allies easily. Another chairman told me that he had several times gone to League meetings with his board's mandate to support Lord if his case was convincing, and each time he had withheld his vote because he found himself offended by Lord's presentation. Lord's election to the League's management committee in 1967, after nine years of trying, has not substantially reduced the vigour of his unquivocal responses to controversy in the game.

It takes a field of fierce and continuing conflict to produce aggression of this order; it is the first characteristic of football that it is always urgent. No one can ever take football lightly in Lord's presence. A man who knows him well once said to him blithely after a match which Burnley had won 4–0: 'Not a bad start to the season, that, eh, Bob?' Lord rounded on his heel and answered, furiously: 'Not *bad*! Is that all you can say?'

This total, humourless concern with what happens to the club has brought Lord into repeated, angry dispute with newspapers and reporters. He is not the only club chairman to be offended by Press handling of news stories about acrimony in football; but no other chairman has ever reacted so violently. Two national newspapers (one Sunday and one daily) and a local weekly paper have been barred from the Burnley Press box, having to report the matches from the stand; six journalists have been banned individually. When I discussed the matter with him one afternoon in 1966, when he was in frank and expansive mood, I found it quite difficult to follow the labyrinthine complexities of the circumstances. What was utterly clear was that Lord was unshakeably convinced that all the newspapers and journalists involved owed him apologies, and that he would not relent until he got them.

His attitude to the Press is not unfamiliar to any journalist who has served his time around football supporters' clubs, local council chambers and trade union offices. It involves a sensitivity to what Lord refers to as 'the power of the pen', and the reference is resentful, slightly envious and always wary. It is the attitude of men who see much privilege in the reporters' access to vantage points and in their freedom to dispose, in a few hundred dispassionate words, of other people's hopes, outrage, anguish, triumph. Lord is echoing the anger of local leaders in other fields, as well as football, when he makes one of his periodic outbursts against reporters' 'interference' in 'private' matters. Burnley's players have been forbidden, on payment of club fines, to talk to the Press without club approval. This has not prevented stories about discontent in the club from appearing in newspapers.

Lately, in the 1967–8 season, Burnley have been struggling in a dispirited alarm. They have had brilliant success under Lord and his manager, Harry Potts, who built firmly on the foundations in team and training that Alan Brown laid for him. But the team which won the championship in 1960 and lost a magnificent FA Cup final against Tottenham in 1962 is now a memory of almost a generation of footballers ago. Burnley, a small town in a scattered region, have always had to rely on home-trained players, because there is not the wealth available to the club of the kind that can be tapped in the great industrial centres. What happens to Burnley will be significant to football, because it will decide whether a club with small resources can continue to hold a place by flair and resolution among the ones which can habitually command massive crowds. Burnley's average gate in the 1966–7 season was 20,500, against Manchester United's 51,000, Leeds' 35,000, Sunderland's 31,000. Burnley will never be able to traffic heavily in the transfer market; their past success has depended principally on retaining an imaginatively blended side. They may sell, but never buy, spectacularly.

Lord's drive and intense commitment to his club have commanded attention. He has been as close as any other club chairman to the figure which is not permitted in British football, the professional director. The man has been true to the setting;

bland dexterity in committee has no value in a club like Burnley. The question now is whether such a man and such a club have not been overtaken by the sheer cost of football at its most competitive. Lord knows exactly what kind of man he is and what kind of football he wants to give his sweat to. He said to me: 'I should never want to be chairman of one of the big city clubs, like the London or Manchester ones. There's too much temptation for the players with all the night-life around. Too much trouble with discipline.' It is the attitude of a chairman who considers every one of his club's problems to be his own.

Neither Needler nor Lord is entirely representative of the British football director in terms of reflecting an average degree of local power; but while both are special cases in that sense, they are common enough figures in age, attitude, local chauvinism and absorption in football. There are many other club chairmen who are diminutives of these two.

The internal politics in which Lord was involved in order to reach the head of the table – the kind of jockeying for position which he has largely prevented during his own reign – occur frequently in other clubs. Ambitious men make their play for position, the most advantageous time being when a club is on the slide; established directors close the ranks or divide in the face of the attack, according usually to the strength of the chairman's personality. The clubs in the strongest position are those whose boards stand collectively behind a trusted manager. His requests for help, perhaps in distant travelling to watch the form of a player he wants to buy, perhaps in looking after the welfare of very young players, focus their attention to a common service. A manager with a squabbling boardroom is like a man with a stomach ulcer, crippled by a nagging distraction.

In the lower reaches of the League, where crowds can sometimes be less than 4,000 a match, directors' personal resources may be vital to a club's survival. In these circumstances directors may pay some of the players' wages out of their own pockets, meet the laundry and the transport bills, or stock a modest bar for the entertainment of visiting directors. Expense like this may be a constant call on them, not just an occasional dip into the deposit account. Between the millionaire chairman, settling money on his team like an indulgent father allowing a favourite son half a dozen birthdays a year, and the small-capital building contractor who pays the centre-forward's wages, there is a bond of affection for football which is more than a lighthearted fondness; the club's need is inescapable to them.

Hunger for dominance, the longing to be associated with success, the pleasure of being applauded for generosity, the dogged attachment to the scene of yesterday's triumph: all these things take men into football club boardrooms. But the game also produces directors who are outside the common syndrome. I have chosen two who are distant in style and background, and also in motive, and who express, I think, the two poles of the football director: Denis Hill-Wood, the chairman of Arsenal, and Ken Bates, the chairman of Oldham Athletic. They are, definitively, the representatives of the public school and Brick Street secondary in the boardroom, the one committed to duty, the other responding to opportunity.

When I asked Hill-Wood if he could tell me exactly when he was elected chairman of Arsenal he said, with the tiniest hint of reproof in his voice: 'You are not elected at Arsenal, you are just asked.' He moved into the chair, he said, 'about six years ago'.

This is the explicit, quite inimitable, English public school
style. It is not a matter of accent but of mould: an absence of
push in the certainty of acceptance; disinterest in trivial detail.
Hill-Wood talks about his family and his own progress through
life like a man taking the Sunday visitors over the stately home,
gently amused at the gawping, and steering curiosity away from
the most private corners with an effortless, kindly switch of
direction.

He was the third of four sons of a Glossop (Derbyshire)
cotton-mill owner, brought up at the time when the wealth of
the north-west cotton kingdom, with its black and castellated
factories, was entering its wane. He was taught his first words of
Greek and Latin, to prepare him for prep school, by his father's
private secretary, who was Harry Stapley, a West Ham and
England footballer. Stapley was in the tradition of the all-
knowing, indispensable Mr Fixits, proper to rich households
of the period: not in the least a below-stairs figure, but a family
confidant. Football was of major importance in the family.
Hill-Wood senior had presented Glossop with a League team
in the way that lesser dignitaries have given municipalities
silver plate. Hill-Wood put it this way: 'I suppose my father felt
it was his duty to give the townspeople something. They had
schools and a hospital, so I suppose he said he'd give them a
football club.'

Glossop was in First Division football for one season and in
Division Two for sixteen. The club faded out of the League
during the First World War. The Hill-Woods left the crumbling
cotton industry round about the same time, and moved south.
Hill-Wood senior was offered a place on Manchester United's
board of directors at one point, but accepted instead the place
offered by one of Arsenal's knights on theirs. Arsenal have
never lacked for gentry in the boardroom.

Hill-Wood's formal education began at Ludgrove preparatory school, which was the one whose joint headmasters were
the two Victorian stars of football we met in Chapter 1,
G. O. Smith and W. J. Oakley. The game was taken earnestly
there, Hill-Wood remembers, and by the time he went to Eton
he was addicted to it. Eton nowadays plays football as much as
Fives, but in Hill-Wood's time it was poorly regarded. He
was, he recalls, the school's only subscriber to *The Athletic
News*, which was a compendious football paper, reporting
every League match in detail, to allow its readers to know,
in Hill-Wood's words, 'exactly how Barrow's inside-right
played'.

It says much for Hill-Wood's determined attitude to the
game that he managed to hold together a team, even if it
sometimes had to be made up in numbers by one or two of the
younger servants. The needle matches of every season were
those against Slough secondary school. (Working-class grad-
uates of Talbot Baines Reed public school literature will know
what relations were normally like between the cavaliers of
School House and the young town toughies, who used to fight
with their feet, if I remember the stories accurately.)

Hill-Wood moved on to Oxford, where he and one of his
brothers both won Blues at football and cricket. They were the
last brothers to win cricket caps simultaneously, said Hill-
Wood, 'until those two Indian chaps, whatever their names are,
did it recently'. After Oxford he played inside-right for Clapton
in the amateur Isthmian League, and reached Arsenal's second
team as centre-forward.

His father, meanwhile, had become one of football's longest
reigning club chairmen. He had taken the chair towards the
end of the twenties, and he held it, 'off and on' as his son says,
for twenty years. 'He stood down now and again for Lord

Lonsdale,' Hill-Wood remembered. This association committed the family to its duty to Arsenal. Denis Hill-Wood was in due course asked to join the board, and since then his son, Peter, has taken his place on it as well.

It was under the first Hill-Wood's chairmanship that Arsenal established their name as one of the greatest football clubs in the game's history. It is a special reputation, which persists even now when Arsenal have little to show in terms of playing success in the living memories of half the fans. The club won the League championship five times and the FA Cup twice during the thirties; but Arsenal's prevailing aura is of metropolitan wealth and glamour, rather than of brilliance on the field. It has to do with the lingering envy and resentment of the provinces, particularly the northern parts, whose football crowds have always enjoyed the crushing of London sides more than most victories. Arsenal were the privileged, all-conquering darlings of London football in that decade before the Second World War which was so bitter for the northern industrial areas, and there is much satisfaction now in trampling on their colours; the pleasure is diminished if they are seen as mediocre opposition.

The present chairman understands this special status. He said: 'People still expect more of Arsenal than they do of most other teams. If one of our players commits a foul the other team's supporters are appalled.' I wrote that comment down with special care, since it was an unusual view of football as recently seen in its most ferocious aspects at Liverpool and Leeds, and Hill-Wood filled the pause with a gentle rider. 'So are we, of course,' he said.

About the time of this interview Arsenal had, in fact, been involved in a succession of particularly ugly eruptions on the field. There had been two matches with Burnley which had

been more memorable for violence than for goals and conse-
quentially subject to disciplinary action by the authorities. To
an outsider Arsenal have looked a distinctly rough-hewn side
in recent years. Billy Wright's inability to raise the level of the
team's play had cost him his job as manager, and his successor,
Bertie Mee, has concentrated on stiffening the defensive resolution to the exclusion of any notable flair in attack. Hill-Wood
insisted that the chairman's job was to be 'head of entertainment'. He said: 'The chairman's got to see that the manager
produces an entertaining side.' Then he qualified this statement
with a flatly pragmatic interpretation of what the word 'entertaining' means in the context of professional football. He said:
'Every fan you ask will say he wants to see lively, open football.
But what the fan really wants is to see his team win.' The
chairman's role was 'to persuade his manager to have a team
which wins approval'.

This urbane, witty stockbroker does not mind at all discussing
the tricky area which lies between the chairman's duty of
persuasion and his temptation towards interference. He hoped
he would never interfere, he said, giving the word heavy
emphasis, 'unless things were going desperately wrong'. On
the other hand his and his board's interest in the club was close,
personal and continuing. Persuasion, when they were convinced
of a certain policy, was not only their right but was required of
them. Buying and selling of players was not something to be
left unarguably to the manager. The directors had to be con-
sulted, and their approval won; they were not prepared simply
to be informed.

Hill-Wood said there was one area in which he hoped he
would do Arsenal a lasting service. He was determined, he
said, that the club should not be left without a capable, experienced assistant manager 'to step in' in the event of the

sudden loss of the man in charge, as had been the case twice before. He thought this loss of continuity in management had been one of the principal reasons for Arsenal's slide out of playing success in recent years. It is difficult to see, though, how this insistence can fail to diminish the dominance of the man in the manager's chair.

Hill-Wood is a courteous, mild-looking man, but his toughness is evident. There is seldom a day when he is not on the phone to Arsenal several times. He travels to most away matches with the League team. He has instituted an intriguing bonus scheme for his players which is based on rewards for long service. It is intended to encourage loyalty as a counter-attraction to the percentages available in transfer fees.

His boyhood, with its stylish affluence, and his everyday setting in the money-dealers' rituals of Threadneedle Street, where men dress for work as if for a rather jaunty funeral (black hats and carnations), make him a curious figure in a game characterized by so much coarse acridity. He fits most oddly in a sport whose more oafish followers like to chant four-letter obscenities in unison and who regard referees with the same bloodshot hostility that they have for railway lavatories. Public school men have been known, of course, to hold farting contests at rugby union matches. Still, this particular Old Etonian would have difficulty in establishing his identity as a football fan if he turned up on the Liverpool Kop.

I asked him whether, had he been someone else's son rather than a former Arsenal chairman's, he would have been likely to be a Saturday regular at League football. He smiled at that, and said he supposed it was unlikely that he would have been a season ticket holder at any professional club. He lives at Basingstoke, which is not exactly in the shadow of any League club's floodlighting pylons. He would certainly have been in football, he said, but perhaps as chairman of an amateur club close to home. The Kop would never understand that a man may not necessarily prefer their football to the amateur kind.

Ken Bates is one of the young, post-war tycoons, impatient with established practice, keenly aware of his own acumen, bold in scope. In a dozen years in business he has added a massive land acreage in South Africa and commercial property in the Caribbean to a capital founded on gravel pits in north-west England. He flies busily about the world, issues peremptory instructions by telephone and cablegram, and his head office is a white-painted, open-planning suite which is the rear section of his elegant old country house in the leafy part of Cheshire. He is a Londoner and sounds it, the voice quick and light. He has a beard, which contributes to a foxy look, and he has an attractive wife and five children. At 38 he has been very rich long enough to be casual about it. He dresses for comfort, with woollen cardigans, before any kind of effect. He no longer belongs to any class except the successful, and he is frank. He became chairman of Oldham Athletic at the end of 1965.

He took over a club 'on its uppers', as he puts it. The crowds at home matches had dwindled to 4,000 people, scattered in little huddles in a ground which had once held over 47,000 to watch an FA Cup match in 1930. There were two rival supporters' organizations, neither effective. There was a strong likelihood of relegation into Division Four at the end of the season. When the club tried to raise money by offering a shares issue Bates bought 19,000 out of the 40,000. He as good as took the place over.

What was particularly unusual in this situation was that Bates had no other connection with Oldham. He had recently been a season ticket holder at Burnley, because he had previously lived near the town. He is a football fan who decided he would like to see what he could do with a crumbling football club if he had charge of it. He chose Oldham because he took a careful look at the field, just as he might in considering the takeover of a string of shoeshops, and decided it was the only available club with the potential to match his ambition.

It was business pragmatism applied to the choosing of a new hobby. He said to me: 'The only way you can usually get into a football club is in times of difficulties. I wanted to be associated with a poor club which had once been successful. That was important because it meant there was the pull among the public in remembering what the club had been like in the great days. But the first requisite was that there should be a large population. In the north-west I decided there were only two clubs which fitted the bill. One was Stockport, and someone else had already got that, and the other was Oldham. Let's be honest about it. What players want to go and live in Barrow?'

He said that when he moved in, the directors making way willingly for him (the previous chairman became vice-chairman), he found a sorry state of affairs. He told me that the bank had refused further credit, the ground was in scruffy disrepair, the manager's 'office' consisted of a desk in the one all-purpose office the club possessed, and 'the *pièce de résistance* was the boardroom – three plastic-topped tables'. He said: 'The public of Oldham had given the club floodlighting which cost £18,000, and it had never even been painted against corrosion.'

The picture, sadly, is not unrepresentative of grounds in the lowest sections of the League, the result of years of decline from the days when habit and the absence of serious competition, in the form of other entertainment, had been enough to fill the terraces with spectators who were never expected to call for comfort.

Bates made rapid changes, laying down a plan for long-term development which he contained in an eight-page memorandum, inclusive of detailed budgeting.

The club, he said to me, had become known as 'a last resting place for old players'. He got rid of twenty-one of them, and the return on the clearance sale was £250, which is now about seven weeks pay for one of his first-team players. At the time I interviewed him he had turned down bids for some of his players totalling £100,000 in the past month. He had been offered £30,000 for one player he had bought for £12,000.

Bates's research had informed him that the average life of a manager with any one League club was two years and nine months. He acquired as his manager Jimmy McIlroy, the former Burnley and Stoke City forward who had a wealth of international experience, and gave him a five-year contract. His innovations, with McIlroy's advice and support, included such disparate methods of boosting the morale of the club as establishing a players' training nursery and fitting the team bus with airliner seats and card-tables. The image he aimed at immediately was of an optimistic club which could offer talented young players the promise of as much reward as could more famous ones.

He applied himself, too, to making the ground far more pleasant for spectators, convinced that he could not expect to attract huge crowds until the distant seasons when McIlroy's long-term training policy would win substantial success. People might be prepared, he said, 'to come and watch a really successful side even if they have to stand up to their ankles in sludge'; but the immediate essential was to bring back a modest crowd by giving them seats, new paint and clean lavatories. He has settled around £100,000 on the club, mostly in stock in his business interests. Ground improvements have cost £45,000.

He has followed the lead of one or two of the more glamorous clubs by offering private boxes to spectators at £25 a seat for the season, and they have been fully subscribed. He has raised all the admission prices by one or two shillings.

His approach did not win total approval in the town. He said: 'When I first went there and started spending money I got letters saying, "God bless you, Mr B., you are our saviour," but when I put the prices up the letters changed. They said, "Go to hell, Moneybags. What do you know about football?" But what encouraged me was that it was the younger people who were on my side.'

He has some scathing words about the entrenched attitudes of some of the older generation. 'What have we got in football?' he said. 'We've got a handful of people flogging their guts out to raise money to subsidize the game so that other people can buy it at less than production cost. People just don't appreciate how cheaply they've had their football. In South Africa the poor starving African is paying a minimum of seven shillings to watch a match.' (Spectators in 1968 could still watch some First Division football in England for four shillings, standing room.)

Bates has brought a sharply commercial mind to the game, accepting that the first principle of business success, the making of money, is not supposed to be an objective in it. The point he makes is that unless football clubs can deal in large sums they cannot possibly expect to reach any major success. To an ambitious club chairman trying to thrust a rundown organization into the top competition profitability must be vital.

His figures on comparative club finances give a dramatic impression of the imbalances in the game. The average Third Division club banks about £1,500 after every home match; the top four or five First Division clubs regularly bank eight or ten times this figure. Yet even with first-team wages at Oldham

F

averaging no more than a third of, say, Manchester United's it still costs £75,000 a year to run Bates's club; United's costs are certainly not ten times that. The gap in wealth between the small League clubs and the biggest ones widens week to week.

Jimmy McIlroy, sitting in shorts and a tracksuit top at his desk after a training session, was cautious about the speed with which his club could push its way up into the limelight. He knew that success would depend primarily on how well his youngsters developed. Among five Irish youths three had been schoolboy internationals and two youth internationals. 'Oldham have never had boys like this before,' he said.

But cash is constantly important, and a bad start to the 1967–8 season, when the team was handicapped by a succession of injuries, reduced the home gates considerably. The average had been nearly 10,000 a game the season before; now it had dropped by 3,500. Bates had announced for public digestion that he had put all the money he intended into the club.

Bates, the London boy turned northern industrialist, has lost the first flush of excitement that his new hobby gave him. He talks, if not gravely about the club, certainly not lightly about it. He dearly wants to make good his assertion that: 'I think we will be in the First Division by 1970 – just by doing the right things consistently, while other dogs are having their day.' Even if he fails he will at least have gathered the satisfaction that comes to adventurous businessmen of his kind from 'giving yourself an opportunity to exercise your own theories'.

This is a different kind of football club chairman from those British football mostly knows. His local involvement is of the instant kind, specially induced for the hobby he has chosen. He would not have taken it if football had not always been at least a variable passion with him; it was only his headmaster's intransigence which kept him off Arsenal's ground staff as a boy. But he has coldly introduced some of the values and methods of the modern business world into a level of football which owes its character to a resolute ignorance of them, and success or failure at Oldham has significance for the sport. He is unequivocal about the situation. 'It is money in the end which makes success,' he said.

4 The Referee

'I've been pig sick when I haven't got a game I thought I ought to have had. I've had to run the line sometimes for someone else when I thought the game was mine by rights. I've said to myself afterwards, "I could have eaten this kid – *eaten* him." But I've still gone to him and shaken his hand, and said, "Well done, son." Well, that's sport. Of course it is.'

The football referee who said that to me revealed much more than the fact that he thought he had not always been sufficiently well rewarded for his sweat. He was speaking for the side of the referee's character which passes barely noticed by either the players or the fans: his place as a competitor in the game.

In English football there are between 15,000 and 20,000 referees. They include boys of 16 and middle-aged men with paunches and inadequate spectacles. Thousands of them never rise above the lowest class of football in those lumbering Sunday afternoon games on the public recreation grounds which ooze tuftily between the lines of council houses and the ring roads. For thousands more there is, at least at some point in their lives, the real hope that they will win their way through to the *élite* eighty, the ones appointed as Football League referees. A few hundred reach the looming obstacle before that happy goal, which is to be accepted as a League linesman; it is from the linesmen that the final promotion to League referee is made.

Referees regard selection for the most glamorous matches, such as FA Cup Finals and international games, with every bit as much longing and pride as do players. The secretary of the Referees' Association talks about the privilege of 'treading the Wembley turf' with as much awe as I have ever heard from any player. Referees suffer from tension before and during matches, as players do; they admit to jealousy and vindictiveness in their fraternity; they become minor celebrities; they receive letters of praise and sour abuse from people they have never met. They see themselves as part of the action, closer to it than managers. Just as with the players, it is when a referee stops getting letters and is no longer being cheerfully booed outside football grounds that he worries most about his future.

On the face of the matter the referee in top-class football is an anachronistic figure. He is still a part-timer, in fact very nearly an amateur, controlling a match in which the players' wages often total £2,000, and the result of the game may hinge on his decisions. Yet he undergoes only a minimal degree of formal training; in most cases he spends the rest of the week in a position of little importance in some employer's office; and he is paid £10 10s a game, with a choice of sixpence a mile or his first-class train fare for travelling, and a £2 10s allowance for staying overnight in a hotel. While football has changed dramatically in terms of pace, competitiveness and anxiety for reward, it is still controlled on the field, where it matters most, from the ranks of the clerks and shopkeepers and foremen who turned to the job when they realised, regretfully, that they would never be competent as players.

The case for and against the introduction of professional referees for the top-grade football will be discussed in the last chapter. Here I want to talk about the nature of the job and of the man who chooses it.

There are a few League referees with substantial professional qualifications in their everyday careers, but most of them have to subordinate ambition, or even effort, in their regular work in order to blow the Acme Thunderer, the standard British referee's whistle, in professional football. Because of the increased speed of the game and the close critical attention nowadays given to refereeing it is accepted that unless a man has reached the League's list of linesmen by his early 30s he will never referee a League match. Every referee must start at the lowest level, and in order to work his way up the promotion ladder, through the town and regional leagues, he must start at the latest before he is out of his early 20s. The League fixes the retiring age at 47.

Maurice Fussey is one of the League's best known referees, attracting attention as much for the obvious jokes that his name invites as by his arresting appearance. He is a tall, galloping-major type of figure, with sparse, sandy hair and a sandy moustache kept uniformly trimmed. Off the field he is relaxed and affable, attentive to questions and ready with inoffensive little stories about the quirks in the characters of famous players and other referees. 'Did you know there's one referee who always takes a hot bath twenty minutes before a game?' he said to me. 'I always tell him it can't be a good thing for his health, but he says it's the only thing that relaxes him.' In action on the field Fussey moves with unforgettable mannerisms.

He is famous for his furious sprints to the scene of dramatic incident. His white knees pump high, and his elbows piston so that his clenched fists jab up and down beside his chin. He is a picture of urgency: authority in a state of tizzy. The crowd often laughs or hoots in encouragement or derision, according to how his decisions have been going for their team. Fussey does not resent this response. For one thing it takes a little of the tension out of the atmosphere. For another his first concern is to reach the spot of the eruption as suddenly as he can manage it, and he does not care that his style is ungainly. He said: 'The thing is that when you blow your whistle for a foul the player's immediate reaction is to turn round and look at you. It's instinct. Now, if you're twenty yards away he's going to argue, because he's got time. But if he turns round and you're right behind him, even if you've just arrived, he's going to think twice.'

Referees are involved in the sweat and the rancour of the game. They are close to the pain and the outrage which can only be observed distantly, and often for that reason imprecisely, by the crowd. Referees are conscious of what the players are saying to each other. They can watch the bitterness develop in a match long before the crowd sees its explosive result.

Referees like to feel that they are respected by players for their astuteness and their fairness; they are, in this respect, like schoolteachers who regard themselves as close to the boys, or police detectives who think that give-and-take with criminals is the best way to deal with them in the long run. Fussey expressed this attitude explicitly when he said, with evident pleasure and pride, that a certain Scottish international player, known for his unpredictable temper, 'doesn't bear me any ill will because I sent him off'. He was confirming the same attitude when he said that another temperamental international 'responds to the right treatment'. This man, he said, was 'a great character, really, and it's no use making a lot of threats'. By and large, Fussey said, he found professional footballers were 'a great crowd', which is generous of him, considering the low opinion players are often prepared to give of referees.

It is striking how closely referees align themselves with players, in contrast with the scorn with which players will detach themselves from connection with the referees. There is no question about who would like to change places with whom. It is a romantic and, it seems to me, most unrealistic view of refereeing to say, as Sir Stanley Rous, the President of FIFA (the international football authority), says: 'It is a job for volunteers, who are doing a service to the country.' Plainly it is not public spiritedness that motivates men into the ambition of controlling big football matches, even if the authorities insist on treating them like servants of duty. As with managers and directors there is undoubtedly a deep absorption in football here, and the material reward is insubstantial to say the least of it. But there is much more satisfying of ego than disinterest in the motive. The referee wants to be recognized in the game, and he wants to feel he is important to it. He even wants to be liked.

Success as a referee requires devotion to the job. A League referee has to keep himself at a level of physical fitness which is far beyond the reach of the average man of his age. In his 40s he has to try to keep close contact with the eye of the hurricane in the game, hard on the heels of the central action all the time. A breathless referee is a flustered and inadequate one, open to abuse from the players and hardly in a position to subdue it. Rous insists that it is vital to the game that 'we should get back to the position we used to have, when players always accepted the referee's decision as final'. The point is that some referees command that degree of submission from players and some are clearly not worthy of it. Fussey, like other leading referees, places physical fitness first in his order of essential attributes for effective refereeing.

He is a bachelor with a clerical job with the National Coal

Board, and his life is centred on football. He trains two evenings and four lunchtimes a week, mostly at Doncaster Rovers' ground, and on the one Saturday in five when he does not referee a League match he trains in the morning and either watches or referees schoolboy football in the afternoon. He began refereeing when he was 21, and it took him eleven years to reach League matches.

Fussey said that he was seldom conscious of crowd reaction, and only occasionally did spectators' abuse get through to him. It needed a lull in the general clamour for the word 'bastard', which was the most frequent epithet, to burn a way through his concentration on the game.

Off the field he wears a large Football League badge on his blazer. Outside grounds on Saturdays, or in the street during the week, he said, people often stopped him to say something like: 'Oh, I remember you. You gave So-and-so a penalty in the Cup in 1962. We'd have won but for you.' The arguments he was mostly called on to settle were those about interpretations of the offside rule. (This rule obsesses some referees as well as spectators. One League referee has named his house 'Offside'.)

Fussey said he was aware of tension at matches but did not think he was unsettled by it. 'But once you step out there you know there's only you who can make the decisions. That's real responsibility, and I feel it. I don't deny it.' When he entered refereeing he was keenly interested, but not immediately imbued with ambition, he said. 'But once I realized I was making progress I knew I had to be a League referee. That was when I got stuck in and really did it properly.'

He named two other qualities for successful refereeing to accompany fitness. A referee ought always to be well turned out, he said, and he had to be naturally tactful: that is, he must not be subject to an impulsive attitude in moments of stress because it immediately angers people. (Is this not the good policeman again?)

There is a standard uniform for League referees consisting of black shorts and shirt, and Fussey said that people were more likely to defer to a man whose uniform was always clean and well pressed. He said: 'It makes him look as if he's going to take it seriously. You're not going to have respect for him if he's in a dirty pair of shorts and some scruffy old shirt.' He adds white shirt-sleeve cuffs to his own uniform. They are an optional extra, which contribute something to the referee's presence and make it easier for the players to see him, he says, when he holds his right arm up. Frozen in that imperious gesture, right forefinger jabbed at the sky, Fussey does not care if he incites the terraces to sniggering as long as he deters the players from disobedience.

The part-timer who disciplines the professionals is in turn judged by the amateurs. The two teams' directors have to report to the League after every match on the referee's performance. Literally, they 'mark his card'. They are required to score the referee on a scale of nought to four: no marks convict him of incompetence, one mark says he is 'poor', two marks or three place him between barely adequate and satisfactory, and the top mark blesses him as 'good'.

Referees are divided on the value of this system. (It is not optional to the clubs; they can be fined £5 for failing to submit a report.) The most self-confident referees tend to defend it by silence, dismissing the matter with the observation that good referees have nothing to be afraid of. Others attack the arrogance of the procedure. Some point to the absurdity of being judged by directors of a team which may have had a couple of penalties awarded against it. The argument in favour of the system says, in effect, that between the views of the most disgruntled directors and those of the most pleased a reasonable mean of a referee's ability emerges over the months. But again the point is glaring that there is a vast difference in attitude between the intense preparation of players to contest the game and the crude, rule-of-thumb manner in which authority oversees it. There is absolutely nothing in the League's regulations which guarantees that the men who are assessing the referees actually know the offside rule.

This is not to say, of course, that there are no clubs which have close connection with refereeing. There are retired referees who become directors, and there are clubs which frequently invite referees to talk to them and their supporters' clubs about the job. But neither the referees nor the League and the FA can influence the clubs in the attention they pay to referees' problems beyond the directors' own degree of interest. The referee is in the unsatisfactory position of a consultant brought in to adjudicate, instructed to brook no interference and then made subject to the criticism of his employers on the grounds that he was not up to the job.

Under these circumstances one of the English referees in the 1966 World Cup, Ernie Crawford, could hardly be said to be overstating the referee's predicament when he said that he needed, above all else, 'a skin like a rhinoceros and to be as deaf as a doornail'. Fire is breathed on him from the crowd, obscenity may be muttered at him by the players, and afterwards he can be accused of both laxity and overzealousness, by directors watching the same game. As Crawford said to me: 'The referee's only got to make one bad mistake and everything else he does in the game is forgotten.'

Crawford reached retiring age after the World Cup, so when

I talked to him at his home in Doncaster he was in the mood to review his career as a referee. It is hard to imagine a more explicit example of a competitor in sport suddenly shoved aside by the years. It was his voice I quoted at the beginning of this chapter, remembering his bitter disappointment at not being chosen for a top game. But his years as a referee had their moments of high flame, as well. He said: 'When you get a letter from Lancaster Gate (the FA headquarters) saying you've been picked to referee a game like England versus Young England, well, the walls move in and out and you could rush outside and kiss people in the street. It's like being picked to play for England.'

Crawford, a tiny Yorkshireman with the unnerving vibratto of the drill instructor in his voice, refereed in ten countries and never thought it necessary, or even relevant, to conceal how much he had enjoyed the glamour and the drama of the exhilarating show-piece matches of international football. His only regret was that he had never taken charge of an FA Cup Final; but in his living-room he pointed out the shining cups and plaques which filled a glass-fronted showcase with a precise memory of each occasion they marked. He took me round the house, lingering at every souvenir with which it was hung. They decorated nearly every wall and corner. There were china plates, dolls, crystal goblets, a gold whistle, a cigar box, plaques and medals, an ornamental bull, vases. Most of them were gifts from foreign clubs or from rich football patrons whose names meant nothing to him. A delicate coffee set reached him from Italy, addressed simply: 'E. Crawford, The Referee, England.' When he refereed in an inter-clubs contest in Barcelona, which had no British connection beyond his own presence, the loudspeakers silenced the crowd with a full rendering of *God Save The Queen*. To mark his selection as a

World Cup referee Doncaster Corporation gave him a blazer with the borough coat of arms on the breast pocket.

Crawford was a League referee for fifteen years. He turned to the job in response to the prompting of one of the elder statesmen of football in his area soon after he admitted to himself that he would never be able to make a living as a player. He remembers his first assignment as a referee in local football with the same cringing pain that some people show when they recall their first visit to a dentist or first fall off a rock face. The match was a local 'derby' between the two teams of the same mining village. 'It was the worst experience I ever had in my life,' he said. He awarded a penalty in the first five minutes. 'I put the ball on the spot and a chap came up and kicked it away. Well, I spoke to him nice and politely and said he shouldn't do that, and that was how it went on. I was dreadful. The game afterwards was just a shambles. I wanted to see a hole in the ground I could jump into. We changed in the pub, and when we got back there the comments were terrible. They paid me five shillings, and they made it up in all the threepenny bits and pennies and ha'pennies they could find. They followed me all the way to the bus, shouting at me.' He was 22.

When he got home he immediately wrote to his mentor, saying that he had refereed his last game. He said to me: 'I told the wife, "I'm not having this, not for five bob a week."' But his anxiety to stay close to football was an ally to authority's persuasion, and his next match was the return encounter between the same teams, the decision made on the same grounds that send high-wire men back up the rope ladder immediately after a fall. He said: 'The advice I was given was to wait for the first chap to open his mouth and then give him some stick. Well, this feller, poor chap, he didn't do anything really, but I tore this strip off him. He didn't know what hit him, and after that it was a wonderful game.'

Crawford reached the League at the time when professional football was still being played on Christmas Day, and he made the point strongly that the privations of referees at the time were far worse than the players' circumstances. A working man without a car in the early fifties, he had to make his own way to Christmas matches when public transport was skeletal. He said: 'This is what I mean by dedication. I've gone to bed at 8 p.m. on Christmas Eve so that I could be up to get the only train on Christmas morning. I've landed up at Chesterfield at 7.30 on Christmas Day, wandering about when there's no one around. I was huddling in this doorway when a policeman came up and wanted to know what I was doing. Well, he had a right. I told him who I was, and he took me off to his little kiosk and we had a cup of tea with some whisky in it. He said, "Well, I thought I had a lousy job, but yours is worse."'

Referees who have worked their way through that sort of thing are not likely to be reticent when they are offering their opinions on the ways other men should prepare themselves for the job. Crawford said he was a frequent speaker at referees' gatherings, and he did not think it could be drummed home too often to them that if they were ambitious they had to train without stint. He said: 'I've run round Doncaster Rovers' track in pouring rain with a towel round my head, when the weather's been so bad that the players have been kept inside for talks.' A referee also needed a sense of humour; he would never succeed if he was pompous; finger-wagging and elaborate lecturing of players could irritate more than control. He said: 'I don't know how many players I've sent off. I don't want to know. It's one of the easiest decisions to make, to send a man

off. That's not what you're there for. The hard thing is to keep
him on sometimes. You do better keeping your voice down.
I've run alongside players and said, "Ee, give over, I knew thee
when tha was a good player." That hurts more than shaking
your finger at a man.'

Crawford was an effective. obeyed referee, probably for the
most part because he remembered his own belligerent nature
as a young player and had the good sense to keep in mind the
fact that youth, impetuosity and the burning will to win go
together in a highly combustible package. He said he had been
'a bad lad' as an adolescent player. 'I'd kick anything above
the grass,' he said. Recalling his own attitude to authority
when he was the age of many of today's professional footballers, he emphasized that all referees should make it a rule
never to touch a player. He said: 'A referee jabbed me in the
chest once when I was playing, and he was the luckiest man
alive. I could have kicked him in the teeth.'

This may not be the tone of voice which the government of
football likes to hear. The leadership suggests, in its public
utterances on the vexing problem of the growing dissatisfaction
with refereeing, that it would prefer a more haughty detachment by referees. This reflects a mistaken belief that the arrogance of authority, as exercised on the school playing field
over a captive company, can be extended to the professional
game as long as the official is enough of a disciplinarian.
Crawford's attitude was that the players knew referees made
mistakes; it was no use pretending otherwise. The task was to
convince the players that the referee always 'gave what he saw'.
Similarly a referee ought to be able quickly to differentiate
between the spontaneous expletives of angered players and the
malevolent abuse of those trying to intimidate him.

Sir Stanley Rous made his name as a referee before he became secretary of the FA and eventually president of FIFA. Admittedly the football Rous controlled was less explosive than today's, but he and Crawford were at one in the view that an adjustable deafness was a positive asset. Rous did not send off the French captain who once questioned the award of a penalty with a furious, 'Bloody *pourquoi*?' Crawford said that there could be little future for the referee who regularly admitted being sworn at; too many complaints would put him in a similar position to that of a player who shows too readily how he can be hurt. Here again we have the point that the referee sees himself as part of the action, not an agent of authority.

Crawford found that the best team captains quickly understood how much it was in their own interests to support the referee; bitterness over a harsh decision might well linger in a captain's mind, but it was less dangerous to his own success than letting one of his men get himself sent off the field for intransigence. Crawford said: 'I've known a captain threaten to thump one of his own men for arguing with me. I always made a point of letting captains I didn't know very well understand exactly what I'd stand and what I wouldn't. I'd say to them "Right, now look, we're going to play football; that's why we're all here. Captains always knew with me that they weren't there just for the toss of the coin.'

In a game which creates as much passion and as much demand on a man's resources as does professional football there are bound to be moments when gamesmanship and outright villainy test a referee to his limit. There are also times when he has to decide which of the two is present in the same incident. The good referee is not the man who plays safe with either a blind eye or a public display of moral outrage, but the one who can unobtrusively remove the teeth from the offence. The story goes that one famous referee awarded a penalty in the closing minutes of a cup-tie, when the score was o–o. As the hot-shot of the visiting side prepared to take the kick the captain of the other team said softly in the hush of the moment: 'Bet you twenty quid you score.' The referee, equally softly, said to the villain: 'Bet you he takes it again if he doesn't.'

5 The Fan

The sound of a big football crowd baying its delight and its outrage has no counterpart. It is the continuous flow of football that excites this sustained crescendo. All other spectator sports are episodic in action: rugby, cricket, tennis, boxing are of their nature each a disjointed series of eruptions punctuated by stoppages which are unavoidable. In football the action is interrupted only by fouls, which add fiercely to the crowd's responses, and when the ball goes out of play, which is very often in the most hectic circumstances.

It is this constancy of conflict that makes football the most satisfying of sports to watch. Because the framework is so simple, so uncluttered, the pictures which fill it can be endlessly varied. The changes are as swift as firelight. Movement adjusts freely to counter-move, restricted only by the minimum of inter-ference of rule. With so little in the frame to dictate method the players are allowed to improvise all the time, and what often results is a complexity of movement of an astonishing invention. Add to this the collisions, the fierce shots at goal, the headlong dives and the majestic clearances from between the posts, and it may be understandable even to the unconcerned who spend their Saturday afternoons combing poodles or in ceramic absorption why men can leave a football match drained of passion. That sudden, damp silence which falls upon a football ground immediately the last players have left the pitch reflects exhaustion. The expression 'football fever' may have been greatly over-used, but it is an accurate description of the condition of the fan when he is at the limit of his excitement. Considering the frequency of his delirium it is remarkable how seldom he injures himself or his neighbour.

The behaviour of football fans has lately alarmed the game's authorities, has invited magistrates to fine and reprove some of the young toughs involved with solemn severity, and has been over-written in the newspapers with more alacrity in band-wagon-stoking than merely mistaken perspective. I am not complaining that individual incidents, such as window-smashing and terrace-scuffling, have been given undue prominence in the papers; viciousness needs to be reported in order that it can be curtailed. But it is irritating that reporters' specific accounts of adolescent oafishness should have become moulded in their offices and subsequently in the public mind into a loose, general, distorted picture of football following gone bad in the root.

Football crowds are never going to sound or look like the hat parade on the club lawns of Cheltenham racecourse. They are always going to have more vinegar than Chanel. But even if thirty-four people were killed in the rioting which followed a match in Turkey in 1967 there is still less danger of physical assault in attending British football than there is in taking a casual stroll round the streets of Johannesburg or New York any night of the week.

The trouble with black ink references to 'ANOTHER NIGHT OF SOCCER SHAME' is that they are deliberately intended to shock rather than inform. They give pleasure to the villainy, who feel they are getting the attention their cuts and bruises deserve, and if repeated often enough persuade a limp kind of public subscription, as with advertisements for goodnight drinks and for the gravy-cubes which are supposed to impart an aphrodisiac to young wives' casseroles. Week by week the Sunday and Monday morning papers suggest a Saturday afternoon scene somewhere between the storming of the Bastille and a civil rights march in Alabama, and round about Wednesday report the squalid little magistrates' court cases which follow the apparent mayhem: three or four skinny 17-year-olds in London, half a dozen more in Liverpool, a couple up in Newcastle, another two or three in Manchester, all pleading guilty to possessing steel combs or knives or to kicking policemen.

This is not say, of course, that there is no cause for worry about violence among football spectators. Unimpeded it would get rapidly worse, like teacher-baiting in the classroom. The problem is to decide two points: how much is it connected with the game, and can the culprits be quelled or kept out of the grounds?

There is no doubt that crowd behaviour is directly influenced by what happens on the field, and that must include anger among spectators as well as humour and bitter dejection. The fan's association with his team is so close that he responds to a game as if to the touch of electricity. But it seems likely that football affects its followers like drink: it disentangles some of their inner nature from the subduing mesh rather than makes them behave out of character. The belligerent become more so, and so do the romantic. But the number of people who are prepared to physically strike someone else, once they have got beyond the age of about 14, is small to say the most of it. For every fan whose feet and fists are loosened by anger there are a thousand who lose control only of their tongues.

Conflict is the essence of football. All sorts of influences come into account when we consider the ways in which different people meet it. There are certainly players who can work on a crowd's emotion much more than others. The crowd noise which accompanies an intricate dribble by a gifted ball-player is very different from that which goes with a shuddering tackle by an uncompromising half-back. Sly players who enjoy tricking opponents into making fools of themselves can produce a sound from the crowd which is unmistakably that of a delighted derision. There are dignified players who are rewarded with hand-clapping, which is nearly as rare in football as swearing at the umpire is at Wimbledon. The point is that most players get exactly the crowd response that is appropriate to their own nature, and this being so it follows that the more bully-boy players there are the uglier will be the conduct among the supporters.

Crowds are not monoliths of equal parts but are composed of infinitely differing personalities. They often congeal, at moments of high drama, into a single voice, but during ninety minutes of a game these components will all flare with pleasure and disapproval at those incidents which strike particularly at their own separate selves. If football were to consist only of delicate, imaginative distribution of the ball, without bodily contact at all, it would be short of a good half of its followers, as it would be if it were played only by the specialists in the tackles which can stun a man. There is no point in arguing about which set of spectators is best for the game; it is part of its greatness that it attracts them both.

I have watched an eruption of bad temper on the field communicate its character immediately to the terraces, the missiles and fists flying in the crowd as soon as the punches were thrown by the players. But I do not think that this kind of spontaneous violence is the kind that need give great concern. This appears to be the impetuousness of angry men, naturally tough, accustomed to a level of aggressive conduct in everyday life on the housing estates and at the shipyard or building site which is unknown to the cricket clubhouse or even the newspaper office. In the posher parts of the ground, where the cigars and the travelling rugs are, the abuse does not get beyond expletives. ('Get that dirty bugger off. Gerrim in the bath,' I heard from very close to a Press box lately, and the tone was exactly the same as that of an argument I heard when I was standing in a packed enclosure at another match and which came as close as a whisker to blows.)

The point about the cheap parts of the ground is that there are a lot of men there who do hard, manual work, and an evident readiness to fight is part of the common coin of social survival among them. The punch-up is threatened far more often than it occurs, of course, just as is the case on the field; players will shake hands at the end of the grittiest games, and so will rival supporters reciprocally back down from their promises to thump each other. You have to stand in among the crowds to realize what the words and the emotions are which sometimes add a special quality of menace to the general clamour of a match. Bearing in mind the state of trembling fury with which some football managers can unburden themselves after a match about referees' decisions which have gone disastrously against their teams, I cannot be surprised that supporters sometimes get kicked or struck on the head with vacuum flasks or beer bottles at moments of furious dispute *during* it. If this were the only kind of violence we were considering there would be less call for the fifty or so policemen who customarily walk a beat round major football grounds nowadays, turning to confront the spectators every time a player hits the ground. But it is not.

The disengaged kind of football followers' violence came into prominence in the later fifties, with the arrival of the train wreckers. Trains, carrying rampaging young fans, would end their journeys with windows broken, upholstery slashed, lavatory fittings broken, the carriages running with beer and crunching under foot with broken glass like gravel. Initially it seemed possible to align the vandalism directly with the disappointment of supporters who had travelled far to see their side go down. Later on it became clear that the result of the game had no causative effect on this kind of behaviour at all: win, lose or draw, there could be trouble or there could be none.

We still have the train smashers (just as we have telephone kiosk wreckers and cinema seat knifers, unconnected with football, although both entertainments appear to have lost appeal in the mid-sixties). But they have been followed by delinquents prepared to make trouble in much closer contact with the game. Shop windows get smashed a few yards from the grounds, and even windows of club buildings. Some of this damage has been done *before* matches. A player has been assaulted by a spectator who ran on to the pitch at Fulham; a referee has been felled by spectators at Millwall. Fighting sometimes breaks out on the terraces when the play on the field is at its most decorous. The lesson seems plain: that not all the culprits in these instances are acting out of excitement for football. Some are using the sport as an opportunity to fight and to damage. They can be so impatient for their own kind of action that if the match does not generate sufficient abandon in the crowd which they can exploit they are prepared to operate without it.

There is evidence that these young toughs go to matches in gangs and that they maintain a kind of rough-house league, seeking out other gangs crammed into the big standing-room terraces and conducting a private war of threats and insults which can boil over into fighting. It is in these scuffles that the knives are produced, and some have been used. The victors in these fights are the gangs which earn themselves reputations for being the toughest in the Football League. Some of these youths are quite ready to explain all this explicitly to reporters and to television cameras, and that is a comment on the general social climate more than one on football.

The trouble here is that the dividing ground between the committed fan with a bit of a temper and the gang member set fair for trouble is also their merging ground. It is difficult, perhaps impossible, to plot the circumstances in which a decent kid from a tough area will be sufficiently influenced by the emotion of the game and the taunts from some visiting toughie to join in the kicking. In the bus taking a crowd of exuberant senior schoolboys and apprentices to a match, rattles crackling and coloured scarves rippling in the slipstream outside the windows, some will have enough built-in checks and balances to keep them out of the scuffles and some may not. What is perhaps most alarming in this business is that the older men in the football crowds, the ones who never run on to the pitch or throw things at the goalkeeper, do not appear to have worked up enough disapproval to deal with the trouble-makers themselves, as I think would have been the case fifteen years ago. The disturbing conclusion is that either they feel outnumbered or they do not really care very much. Again this situation is reflected in wider scope elsewhere in contemporary social life: we more often seem to be afraid of our young than influential upon them.

I am not going to be popular in some quarters by saying here that I believe more people than are prepared to admit it take a surreptitious pleasure in this display of oafish anarchy on the football terraces. I remember in my own case a few years

ago feeling some exasperation with Authority when it used to
get worked up into a red-faced bluster about the criminality
of small boys who would rush on to the pitch at the end of a
game to gather round players. But I can see now, although I
am not at all sure that this was the reason for Authority's
outrage, that this kind of licence may well lead on, as if
naturally, to the kicking and bottle-throwing by adolescents.
The agents of discipline in every sphere are unpopular nowadays: the reactions against the impending doom of adulthood
and the wastelands of the housing estates are complex, but what
is plain is that they find relieving expression in turmoil. People
enjoy watching violence, and they are fed it in children's
comics, in pop music and by the cinema and television. When
it occurs on the football terraces there is relish as well as con-
demnation in the way the seated ranks and the newspapers
respond to it.

There have been some glaringly ugly outbreaks of brawling
in the 1967–8 season, most notably the scenes which followed
the explosive match between Celtic of Glasgow, and Racing
of Buenos Aires in Montevideo, when five players were sent
off the field, and those after another Celtic game, this time
against Newcastle United, when a total of fifty-seven people
were arrested. Neither match had any history of inter-club
rivalry behind it, the one at Newcastle being a so-called
'friendly' contest and the Montevideo game being the final of
the World Club Championship, which pits the European
champions against South America's. It looked as if the offending
Celtic followers were at Newcastle defending their reputation
for toughness, and in just the same spirit in which groups of
louts from Glasgow or Liverpool will throw their weight about
in the presence of London East Enders encountered on holiday
at Blackpool. This kind of thing is not new to Britain or to any

other country: it is just a preposterous, brutish version of regional loyalty – urban, adolescent tribalism. Football has called heavily on local involvement, and always will. Having raised the banner of town chauvinism, and prospered under it, the clubs have total responsibility to restrain the over-committed and to expel from the ranks the vicious joined only for the pillage.

The question is how? Certainly if all players behaved decorously more spectators would; or, to put it another way, there might well be fewer of the kind of spectators who do not wish to. But mildness of manner on the football field is never going to be a general condition, not in any class of football let alone the most competitive kind with which go the top prizes, the top wages, the biggest crowds and the most persistent crowd trouble. I have written in the past, in the *Observer*, about the contribution some petulant or bullying players make to the eruptions in the crowds, and the point is still being demonstrated by the week. But this applied twenty years ago, in my own memory, and from others' a long time before that. It may be useful to divorce players' violence from spectators' in considering how to quell both kinds, while admitting a past correlation. Players' behaviour is for another chapter. I will leave that matter here for the moment with the observation that arrogance and combativeness will always exist in football, and it may be realistic to accept a level of it in the crowds which is consistent with that among the players. It is the premeditated, gang forms which need to be systematically removed if the game is not to be cripplingly disfigured in the future.

It seems inescapable that the two critical problems are the adolescent age group and the layout of nearly all football grounds. Except by some extreme methods of screening at the turnstiles, by which the 16- to 21-year-olds would simply be refused admission, which would be grossly unjust to thousands of the blameless, there is no foolproof way of keeping the trouble-makers out of the grounds. But there seems no reason why a rigid enforcement of rule by the police, engaged by the clubs to look after their private property and their patrons, should not weed out the delinquents much more effectively once they are inside the grounds than is done at present. Policemen on the 'in' side of the turnstiles could well take aside the suspicious-looking character with the bulging pockets and the metal-studded belt for a thorough examination. The known villain could be banned from the club by the club, in the same way that he is banned from public houses by the landlords. This sort of operation would obviously call for more policemen; it might call for a form of the private riot squad as seen at certain political meetings – and even certain religious ones.

Is this unpleasant? Does it have fascist overtones? The answer is a deeply regretted 'yes' to both questions. But the culprits are calling the tune. There are not many of them yet; unless they are eradicated in their present small number there could be too many of them to be handled a few years from now. The fact that much of the trouble they cause occurs outside grounds does not mean that it can only be stopped there. They have chosen football as a tailormade area for their activities. Its atmosphere is ripe for them, so is its physical setting. If they are deterred from travelling to grounds, fairly sure that they will not be able to get in, they may well take their aggressions and their bottles somewhere else. That would be unfortunate for the new objects of their attention but they are more damaging to football than they might be to less congested settings. Dispersal is half the battle.

Suggestions like these are not unknown to the clubs. It is deeply disappointing, to say the least of it, that so few clubs have chosen to act positively on them. They have prevaricated on the grounds of expense, of the difficulty of organization, of taking mountainous measures to cart away molehills. But the real reasons for their reluctance to act in such ways are nearer to cowardice than to a sense of proportion. They fear the fickleness of supporters; they fear that disgruntlement over the inevitably harsh treatment of some innocents, to say nothing of the guilty, might reduce public affection for the team; they fear that there might be reprisals by the excluded. On a more general, emotional plane, they wonder whether too much tampering with the tumult of football following might diminish it substantially in the public concern.

The fears are not groundless, but they are being allowed to overrule the larger interest of the future of the sport. It might well be that many people would be repelled by the sight of hefty policemen, official or otherwise, seizing on lads apparently intent on cheering on their football side and bundling them off to the makeshift cells below the stand: a nasty thought indeed. But unless some strictness in admission to grounds is introduced those same people are going to be repelled from the game in any case, and by the kids not by the policemen. The clubs' duty is surely to protect the game and the fans, and at the moment not many of them are making much attempt at it.

Most crowd trouble comes from the standing areas behind the goals, as any 10-year-old fan will tell any club chairman. Most standing areas behind the goals are terraced in very much the same way in which they were built in the days when youths did their brawling in the yards of back-to-backs rather than at football matches. These massive staircases, as at the extraordinary Kop at Liverpool's ground, have a unique place in the history of British football. They have become over the years some of the privileged places of working-class communion.

For those of us who first learned our professional football jammed against the crush barriers down at the bottom of them, having arrived hours early to establish a position of comparative safety rather than submit to the baby protection of the boys' pen, they are more evocative of the wonder of childhood than even old comic-strips are. They are hideously uncomfortable. The steps are as greasy as a school playground lavatory in the rain. The air is rancid with beer and onions and belching and worse. The language is a gross purple of obscenity. When the crowd surges at a shot or a collision near a corner flag a man or a boy, and sometimes a girl, can be lifted off the ground in the crush as if by some massive, soft-sided crane grab and dangled about for minutes on end, perhaps never getting back to within four or five steps of the spot from which the monster made its bite. In this incomparable entanglement of bodies and emotions lies the heart of the fan's commitment to football. The senses of triumph and dejection experienced here are never quite matched in any seated section of a football ground. It is the physical interaction which makes the monster the figure of unavoidable dreams it becomes.

To kill off this animal, this monstrous, odorous national pet, would be a cruel act of denial to us. The goal-end terrace, Kop or Cow-shed or Stretford End – any fan can name one – is as much part of the British game as is the memory of Matthews or the present genius of Best. Yet it is here, where the love of the game is fiercest, that the louts with the pimples and the knives have embedded themselves. They choose the points where they are farthest from the law, and, it has to be admitted, where the climate is most favourable to them. It is here where adjustments to the layout of crowd accommodation need most urgently to be made.

The clubs have to find a compromise between a stultifying

orderliness on the terraces and a deference to their traditions. Some clubs have already begun work, adding to the number of crush barriers and rearranging them so as to break up the concentration of people and make it easier for police and officials to move among them. But the problem is not a light one, and not nearly enough imaginative thought is being put to it. There are clubs which have spent lavishly on new seating tiers, in one or two cases achieving a distinctive architectural handsomeness previously unknown to British football except at Wembley. Has any club asked an architect to create a new style of goal-end terracing? There must surely be architects among the ranks of the clever-headed, post-war workers' boys who have grown up with football in their veins and who would relish the challenge of such a task. I am thinking in terms of something altogether less sombre, less squalid than the terraces we have: something which would not merely facilitate freer movement for the disciplinarians but might also take some of the meanness out of the environment.

I certainly have no wish to see imposed a planner's end to honest rancour and loyalty, just because they are coarsely expressed: the merchants of blandness are already legion enough. But it ought to be possible to preserve the circumstances of excitement while doing away with the opportunities for viciousness. In fact, it is vital to.

Mostly football crowds control their emotional fury themselves, turning on their own cooling sprinklers of humour when the heat rises dangerously close to the intolerable. I remember in boyhood the lone, amazing voices thundering out of the general din at Wolverhampton Wanderers' matches, rough-edged Chaliapins clearing the chorus, telling the referee to use his lamp (a miners' allusion to short-sightedness) or a trailing

fullback to get a bus. Referees were let into the secret the world
had been keeping from them that they had heads like swedes.
Wingers were informed that they couldn't run a raffle, and
linesmen asked if they wanted a lift with the weight of their
flags. It was spontaneous, aggressive stuff in the wit style of the
workers' bus and the tea-break. It is only in the sixties that the
crowds have turned to the rehearsed chants and verses which
now add a strangely disciplined texture to the improvisational
din. We have a plainsong of the terraces.

It was created in Liverpool, where the city character, with its
pervading harshness of waterfront life and bitterly combative
Irish exile content, was given a sudden flowering of arrogant
expression with the simultaneous rise of its pop musicians and
of both its leading football teams. More than any other English
city, Liverpool experiences its hope and its shame through its
football. There is no more chilling sound in the game than one
of the long howls of animosity which the Liverpool crowd can
drill into the ears of a visiting threat to their club's supremacy,
such as Manchester United or Tottenham Hotspur. Anfield,
Liverpool's ground, and Goodison Park, Everton's far smarter
one, can give voice to collective vindictiveness in a way that
no other English crowd can match. The Liverpool crowd is
consistently the more obscene of the two, the Kop sometimes
achieving a unison with four-letter words which drums in the
head like a sock in the ear from a mallet. On a wet day, with
the steam and the cigarette smoke hanging grey and yellow in
the air, and the derision exploding in wicked humour out of
this gloomy cavern, the Kop has all the menace of an hysteric's
nightmare.

The Kop's jokes can be cruel, but they can also show a
surprisingly subtle awareness of the crowd's own nature. In
a match against Everton, in which Everton's international

centre-forward, Fred Pickering, was seriously hurt and had to
be carried off, the Liverpool fans' chant went: 'Dead Fred,
Ha, ha, ha.' You can't get more relishing of the enemy's mis-
fortune than that. Yet in a game at Anfield against Manchester
City there was an arresting moment when Doyle, City's young
wing-half, falling against one of the corner flags under the Kop
and uprooting it, silenced the laughter by picking the flag up
and playfully lunging with it at the crowd. There were some
moments of muffled consultation, and then the Kop burst out
with a massive chant of: 'Hoo-li-gan, hoo-li-gan.' The Kop
is not a members' enclosure at Ascot, and nor does it regret
it.

Nor is it composed entirely of beery Liverpool partisans blind
to every talent unless it comes in an all-red strip. I once reported, in some irritation after a particularly bleak game at
Anfield, that it was not permitted on the Kop to congratulate
the opposition. It was too comprehensive an accusation. The
insertion of the word 'seldom' would have given it accuracy,
and it would certainly have reduced the abuse which inevitably
followed. One correspondent condemned me as a writer of
'rubbish', but outdid my own mis-hit with the statement that
'the fame of the Kop is largely due to their fair treatment
of opposing teams', which is like saying that Cassius Clay's
boxing reputation is largely due to the generosity he shows
after fights to his victims. Another reader, advising me that
he had been a patron of the *Observer* for as long as he could
remember and that he was 14 years old, admonished me with
a most dignified assurance that good work by the opposition
was never allowed to pass unrewarded by him and his col-
leagues.

Well, I do not deny that the very best of opponents at Liverpool, particularly brilliant forwards, are applauded now and

again amid the fire of intimidation, but unstinted congratulation of visiting teams arises from the most special of circumstances. The two most memorable occasions in my experience both involved Hungarian teams. Hungary's World Cup side, defeating Brazil 3–1 at Goodison, was thunderously acknowledged for its attacking invention by the crowd, which rose to the centre-forward, Albert, with such munificence that Albert lifted his water-bottle to them from the end of the players' tunnel in reciprocal salute. Again, when Liverpool were knocked expertly out of the Fairs Cup competition by Ferencvaros of Hungary, the impeccably balanced inside-forward Varga slicing the home defence with an assassin's stealth, the Hungarians' overall flair and certainty of touch were seen plainly for their full worth and the Kop stayed on at the end to *clap* them from the field. I have italicized the verb because the Kop does not do much clapping, and the gesture looked to me to be a pointed comment aimed at the Liverpool management as well as applause for Ferencvaros.

Vivid memories are frozen in my mind of crowd scenes at Liverpool's and Everton's grounds: the sight of a small, ragged boy appearing on the skyline of the Kop's acutely slanting roof, stepping gracefully down to the middle of it and sitting down, arms folded, a tiny, symbolic representative of the bravura of his people; also a scrambling invasion of the Goodison Press seats on the Saturday when Everton made sure of the League championship, my fingers flattened beneath the foot of a triumphant fan determined to pay his respects to the directors' box.

It was, of course, a Merseyside fan who ran the length of the Wembley pitch, was seized by a policeman and wriggled deftly free, leaving the policeman with nothing to remember the man by but the coat he left in his hands. And it was, of course, the

G

Merseyside crowd which first gave a clearly enunciated rendering of 'God Save Our Gracious Team' in the presence of royalty.

The Liverpool crowds have been imitated, but never adequately, no other fans being able to match the invention, to say nothing of the sustained indecency. Chants of 'We Are the Champions' from ragged choruses of down-the-table team supporters irritate more than excite. Musically, Manchester United's fans score well with a convinced singing, to a popular South American tune, of 'Eee, aye-aye-aye, *Charl*-ton is *Bet*-ter than *Pel*-ly'. There is not a crowd in the League now which lets us get away from a game without at least one chorus of 'Eee-aye-addio, the Goalie is a Queer'. But the Kop can always go one better. 'Where's Yer 'Andbag?' it asks visiting goalkeepers as they hunch in the goal before it.

Fans are wealth to a football club, yet until the most recent years they were largely ignored except when they were inside the ground. Even now the interest clubs take in their supporters appears to depend more on need than success. Most of the clubs with recently developed supporters' social amenities attached to them, rather than supporters' own clubs independently organized, are those which made a bid for renewed support simultaneously with their efforts to drag themselves out of decline and into prominence as playing forces. Both Coventry City and Manchester City, as cases in point, invested heavily in social facilities for fans at a time when both were struggling to thrust out of the doldrums of the sport. The Manchester enterprise represented an investment of about £100,000, with a club close to the ground which is open seven days and nights a week and which pays in a clear profit to the football club of around £14,000 a year. That sum, of course, would not buy any one player of proved ability in the First Division; but it takes care of some of the football club's day-to-day running costs, and it represents in terms of the social club's customers who have made it possible a continuing, direct link of interests.

Talking to members of City's social club, I was told with much delight that they had never before felt so involved with the footballers they had watched over the seasons. Players, club directors and the management went to the social club frequently, not only to give talks and to comment on football films but just to be in contact with the fans and available for conversation.

It has always been obvious that this kind of contact is highly prized by football fans, and it is astonishing that so few clubs have tried to use the fact to their own advantage. The huddles round players' entrances before matches, people just hoping for a close-up glimpse and perhaps a rub of shoulders with the heroes, reflects this avidity for the privilege of casual association. Taken a couple of steps forward, so that the fan turns up one evening in his club for a pint and is allowed to buy a bitter lemon for the goalkeeper, the pleasure is cemented into a lingering pride. 'I was talking to So-and-so last night,' the supporter can tell his mates at work the next morning, dropping a star player's name like a matchstick, and he is conscious of importance. As one of the social club members said to me, 'I feel part of things. I've been watching City for fifteen years, and until this year no one had ever suggested I'd ever meet a player. I think it's a great thing.'

For this kind of man, aged 38, a toolmaker with a decent regular wage and an insatiable appetite for football, the sense of involvement with his team is a sense of indebtedness. This kind of fan, who travels to every away match and who is appalled at some of the misconduct which has developed on the terraces, is the lifeblood of football following. Well informed about football, a keen player as a boy, totally committed to the side which circumstances chose for him, he said that his wage of roughly £22 a week enabled him to see all the football he wanted and also to go away for an annual holiday; but if his money were to drop he would cut first the holiday and then probably his beer before he would countenance curtailing his football following. 'Well,' he said, 'a young nephew of mine asked me if I'd try to get Tony Coleman's autograph on a picture he'd got of him. Coleman took it into the dressing-room and got all the team to sign. You can't ignore something like that.'

This man, well built, said he had sometimes been involved in shouting arguments with supporters of other clubs, usually concerning who was or was not a dirty player; but he had never been threatened with violence or ever felt he was likely to be. In his conversation about football the violence on the terraces was very much a peripheral, if shocking, curiosity.

The economics of his football were fairly elastic within their small scope: less than £1 for an away match, probably sharing petrol costs with two or three friends, if the town was in Lancashire or Yorkshire; about £3 10s for a London game, the little group going carefully on food and drink. It is worth remembering how narrow is the gap between scrimping and extravagance among the people who make up the bulk of football crowds; it may help richer men to understand why there is so much bitter, sometimes inflammable, disappointment among supporters who have watched their side crushed a very long way from home. The man I was talking to felt well served by life: he could afford his football, and he had seen a child's eyes shine when he could say he came hot from City's dressing-room, or at any rate from as close as most people get to it.

The football fan is not just a watcher. His sweat and his nerves work on football, and his spirit can be made rich or destitute by it.

6 The Amateur

The Football Association estimates that very nearly a million amateurs, outside of schools, play in organized football in England and Wales. Whatever some of this football may look like to the casual watcher, who comes upon it when lost in some suburban maze of pebbledash in a Sunday afternoon drizzle, it is no light matter to the players.

There are, of course, a large number of smart, well-appointed amateur clubs, with neat little grounds assiduously groomed, which train their players diligently for regional tournaments and for the national Amateur Cup – whose final attracted 75,000 spectators to Wembley stadium in 1967. But for the majority of this army of amateurs football is a contest in the mud of public recreation grounds, with a dozen little brothers and goose-pimpled girl friends to shout them shrilly to victory, or defeat, by amazing margins: St Cuthberts 13 – Coach and Horses 1, Cherry Tree Bus Depot 0 – Activated Sludge By-products 12. This football is as much a compulsion to its players as is the First Division to its fans.

A visit to one of England's massive Sunday football fields, say London's Hackney Marshes or Manchester's Hough End, ought to be included in the itinerary of every overseas intellectual who comes to the country under the auspices of Education to examine our character and locate our points of tension. These fields, crammed with football pitches so that perhaps twenty matches are being played simultaneously in exclusive absorption, reflect with glaring clarity the aspect of the British nature which the rest of the world fails generally to perceive: our obsession with prolonging physical competitiveness. We cherish the fact of youth with singular anxiety, resenting its flight even more than we do our weather. Our stubbornness in the face of advancing years is not a graceful characteristic, but it is a dominating one. In manly company references to So-and-so as a wicked old devil or a tough old beggar or a cunning old sod are essentially admiring: age is stressed to make the point that it is not hampering the man's activity, whether this is drinking or fathering children or scoring goals. Sustained sexuality is a matter of pride in any society; but no other country I have been in likes to parade its preserved vitality through sport as much as Britain does.

Perhaps unconsciously we are reacting individually against our decline, in our historical old age, as an international force. I have watched sport, organized and casual, in many countries; none of them can match the percentage of bald heads and paunches and gaunt ears, and all the other unwanted gifts bestowed by the old man with the scythe, that can be seen on Britain's cricket grounds, squash courts, tennis courts, football fields – above all, on the football fields.

At Hough End, a great, low-lying urban plain off one of Manchester's major entry-and-exit roads, the grass bordered on one side by a railway line and on another by a prefabricated housing estate, the goalkeepers line up back to back, only ten yards separating one line of pitches from another. Old warriors conserve their wind by playing wily midfield games, suppressing criticism from younger men for their immobility by shouting the loudest and lacing compliments with baritone abuse of referees, often younger than themselves. The pitches are so

close, side by side, that the balls whiz muddily from one game
into another, striking wingers distractingly as they gather
themselves for a subtle centre into the opposition's goalmouth, startling referees into involuntary blasts on the whistle,
whacking spectators in the back of the neck as they scoff
knowingly at imitations of the bolt defence and the 4–2–4
formation. Escaped poodles frisk among the players' legs,
and lads with Rolling Stones haircuts collide with static
veterans like gollywogs flung against a nursery wall. Some
of the recrimination tells touchingly of the aching confrontation of Narcissus with his beer-barrel tummy: 'What
d'yer mean, *run*? I've *bin* running. For Christ's sake, *roll* the
ball.'

A team manager with a grey crew-cut and a shortie overcoat
told me he knew one old player who had grown so decrepit that
no club would give him a regular game; but he turned up week
after week with half a dozen jerseys of different colours in his
bag, hoping to get a game with any team a man short. I
watched an inside-forward collapse very slowly, contracting
and wrinkling before our eyes like a balloon still hanging on the
Twelfth Day of Christmas, when the ball struck him in the
middle of his stomach, bulging under his yellow jersey. The
other players grouped solicitously as he knelt on all fours and
waited for his pulses to judder into life again.

Some of these old players, who may be well into their forties,
have known big crowds and skilful football. They are treated
in the main with little deference, dismissed by younger men as
'old crocks – knee jobs, mostly'. But if you watch carefully you
can spot a sudden flare of a talent beyond the normal: a quick
ground pass which leaves a defence with its backs to the ball,
or a feint and a little sprint which takes a fat man or one with
scarred knees yards clear in a moment. Such things are properly

acknowledged by surrounding players and spectators: 'Eee,. Rodge, I told yer to watch that old bugger.'

Having been an obsessed boy footballer and being now an obsessed spectator, I sympathize totally with these men who are so reluctant to go under to the assault of time. In fact, at the age of 34 I allowed myself the senseless indulgence of playing in a football tournament when I had not kicked a ball in earnest for around fifteen years. I considered myself fairly fit, because of frequent mountaineering, admittedly of a gentle sort, but I had not bargained for the effects of two aspects of football which the very young never have to consider: the necessity for sustained running and the repetition of sudden movements to right and left.

The tournament was for six men to a team and for fifteen minutes play each way, but the calamitous mistake was in the use of a full-sized pitch. I delivered shortly after the fifth minute, when the grass was already undulating in waves of nausea before my eyeballs, a long, low pass of exquisite accuracy into the stride of an Australian forward who failed miserably to read my intention. I turned on my right foot with impetuous disgust and felt an alarming pain on the inside of my right thigh. Rendered incapable of any further devastating sprints and swift switches of direction, I spent the rest of the game in goal.

There was a fateful inevitability about this situation, because the prospect of goalkeeping always frightened me in the days when I played regularly and I suffered a secret dread that there might one day be a match when I would have to stand between the goalposts to face some kind of climactic onslaught upon my courage. The moral of this story is that the flying winger aged 13 is a more thrilling figure in the memory twenty-one years later than he is in resurrection. There are thousands of ageing footballers who know the lesson well enough; they simply choose not to heed it.

It intrigues me and satisfies me nowadays to observe that the English schoolboy still rebels against any attempt by authority to obstruct him from football just as my own generation did. It pleases me out of all proportion to the local significance of the circumstances to watch organized rugby at a school near to my home change instantly to improvised football the moment the teacher's back is turned.

I remember clearly the bitter sense of imposition I used to feel at being made to pick up, and run with, that ridiculous ball with its pointed ends, when I could kick a round one naturally. I have always felt that compulsory school rugby in any area where football is the paramount sport – and that means just about every town outside South Wales which has any pretension to being an industrial employer – is an infliction of crass snobbery. It is even bad for rugby, because it brackets a good game with other foisted and incomprehensive chores like boiling things in test tubes and multiplying the first letter of the alphabet by the second.

It pleases me, too, to note that among amateur teenage footballers the brilliantly ostentatious gear which I and my friends always wanted to wear is still equally desired; and now, which is the difference between our two generations, it is available. Today's public park football is not that raggle-taggle scene of working clothes and hand-me-down strips flapping about kids' bodies like institutional pyjamas. The younger teams dress up in some show, outdoing even the continental professionals in brevity of shorts and vividness of colour. Shiny red shorts go with red and black shirts, there are shirts in gold and green quarters and there are gold shorts with blue numbers on them and gold shirts with white shorts. There is a touch of Carnaby

Street to go with the squelching mud and the truculence, but this arresting plumage does not invite any questioning of masculinity or resolution. One team secretary, who told me his players bought new colours every year, said: 'I say to my lads when we see a side come on in a smart outfit, I say, "Right, lads, this lot look formidable."' The gear is part of the romance of football, part of the special ambience of privilege that goes with being picked for a team.

These amateur sides often operate without any kind of premises of their own. They may centre on a church club, a factory department or a pub. They have to maintain at least a loose form of organization to qualify for registration with the FA, if they want to take part in any of the recognized competitions. But the authorities recognize that a club may not materially consist of more than the fifteen or sixteen names from which the team is picked every week. Club night may be nothing more elaborate than a general conversation in one of the public rooms in a pub, Sunday's team selected between drinks and impromptu darts matches. Many players turn out for one such little club on a Saturday and another one on Sunday.

It is one of the strengths of the loose but encouraging organization of amateur football in Britain that thousands of groups of this kind can thrive with a minimum of contact with officialdom. Authority used to be more pompous than it is now, withholding its recognition from Sunday footballers. But the FA accepted the affiliation of Sunday clubs in 1960, and as a result there has been a tremendous increase in the number of people playing in properly run tournaments, even if some of the refereeing (to say nothing of the changing facilities) is of the rough and ready kind. The important point about all this football, varying so much in quality and effort, is simply that it is being played. Hackney Marshes and Hough End display a lot more animation in our bleak urban fastnesses than foreign readers of the *New Statesman* might be expected to imagine.

Among the more skilled of these little clubs there can be found the devotion to football, and that abiding ambition in it, which I have said before is central to British industrial life. I spent an evening with a pub team which played in the Salford Sunday League, and which I picked out at random for no other reason than that its name appealed: the Pied Piper. We sat around a table drinking pints of mild and ran our minds over the list of players. The left-back had played trial games for Birmingham and Stoke City, the left-half for Huddersfield and Bury, the centre-forward for Manchester City and the outside-left for Bolton. Two more of the team were 20-year-old twins who had spent their first two years out of school on Portsmouth's ground staff and playing for one of the club's youth teams. The crowd used to call them Pinky and Perky.

I asked the group how many of them had wanted to be professional footballers, and after a silence in which the players looked at each other as if they had been spoken to in French, the centre-forward replied: 'Well, every lad does, doesn't he?'

7 Football and the Press

At the age of 17 I was confronted with my first ethical dilemma in the reporting of football. Under the subtle pseudonym of *Linesman* I used to report Stafford Rangers' semi-professional matches in the Birmingham Combination, and if that particular competition sounds remote and trivial to some readers they may like to note that its weekly games could frequently command 4,000 spectators, which is more than some Fourth Division clubs can say nowadays. I used to travel in the team bus, along with my rival on the town's other weekly newspaper, who was the same age as myself and wrote under the name of *The Cobbler*. We were treated with a rough, amused kindness by the manager and the directors, and we took our jobs with the utter earnestness that went, in the late 1940s, with about £2 10s a week for somewhere around ten hours' work a day. I am looking, as I write this, at a long, thin cutting which I have just extracted from the pages of a diary for 1948, and this example of my work of the period gives a fair illustration of the degree of detail which was expected of us. The report opens like this: 'Stourbridge kicked off and attacked strongly, but their raid ended when the ball went out for a corner.' You cannot get much more austerely factual than that.

The critical moment came at an important away match, when our team was found to be a man short; I am not certain now whether the reason was an injury or the complications intrinsic to travel at the time. The gap was filled by the club's youngest director, who assumed the persona of the missing player named on the programme. Now this was illegal, since the director was not a registered footballer. It was also a good story. The club chairman took *The Cobbler* and me gravely aside and confided the information, achieving a rare mixture of dignity and helplessness as he threw himself upon our loyalty to the town and asked us to conceal the frightful deed from the public, and from Authority. The director played like one. *The Cobbler* and I hid the facts from the other reporters in the Press box and discussed our duties and moral obligations all the way home.

We put the matter to our editors on Monday morning, and after a great deal of head-shaking and wrestling with consciences we suppressed the story. We did not actually lie. We mentioned neither the director nor the missing player. We did not list the teams at the end of the report. There were, of course, numerous letters from readers, questioning this unprecedented omission, and none of them got a satisfactory answer. Without a doubt the Press had been gagged, even if by consent. I think it was the consent that troubled me most. I always felt an uncomfortable sense of compromise in the team bus after that, and reacted to it by being more sharply critical of the players' deficiencies. Their form became 'unpredictable', and even improved performances were qualified as 'much needed'. Only the arrival of National Service in khaki broke the gathering conviction of moral turpitude. Ah youth, or something.

It is to be hoped that this dark confession does not bring calamity upon Stafford Rangers at a distance of twenty years from the offence. I am bound to say that the matter does not appear exactly horrifying at this remove. I have, after all, watched people starving to death in the interim. I have plucked the comic little skeleton from its cupboard because it is a neat account of the special relationship which can exist between football and the Press. If we consider The Game at its widest, to include club clerks, mascots, fans, and not only players and managers, newspaper reporters are integral and very important to it. The nature of their association with the clubs is strongly reflected in the way they write about the sport. People are seldom objective about sport, least of all about football; the appeal to aesthetic awareness, to emotion, to a man's sense of injustice, to his capacity for self-identification, results in complex responses, and the reporter is not excluded from these just by putting a ball-point pen in his hand.

There are some reporters who are much more like public relations officers for particular football clubs than others. Reporters with provincial papers, and even one or two of those on national ones, are commonly assigned to follow particular clubs almost everywhere they go. The mere preservation of a tolerable social connection between such a man and the club's players and officials means that he is unlikely to be uncompromisingly critical of them. There is no suborning implied here, but there is a combination of day-to-day friendliness and professional ingratiation. Such a reporter comes to view his assigned club rather as some motoring correspondents treat the new cars they are invited by the manufacturers to test: the acceleration is magnificent, the road-holding superb, but what a pity the ashtrays are so small and the rake of the rear passengers' seat not all one could wish. Following a football club as its Boswell week after week over several years may establish a reporter's local standing, may inform him in the most privileged way about players' quirks and directors' cunning, but it may also diminish his readiness to give offence.

One has only to sit in a Press box when a Scottish club team is playing an English one to note this partisan alignment of reporter with club at its most obvious. It is noticeable at international matches, when foreign journalists frequently abandon any pretence at professional objectivity in the face of belligerence on the field. This kind of immediate, bold identification is scaled down a bit among the travelling reporters close to, say, a north-east of England team or a London one, playing another English club, but it still often applies. Along with the invaluable information they will generously share about players' ages and villages of birth goes an unavoidable aura of the representative.

This situation is inescapable in a commercial, competitive Press. Readers' interest in football is insatiable, and it has been found to be intense at the level of chitchat. Newspaper circulations at their biggest are sustained by the unbroken flow of trivial detail as well as by occasional sensation. Who is on the treatment table for half an hour because of a minor strain? Who's wife has had a baby? Who's moved into a new house with double glazing? Who's son is four on Cup-tie day? Who cares? Millions, it seems; and these questions can be answered only by reporters in constant, relaxed contact with the clubs.

Football does a lot better out of this flattery than it admits. The clubs have grown so accustomed to this fussing, innocuous attention that the publication of unpleasant detail can sometimes send them into retaliatory outrage – outrageous, that is, in both senses of the word. There has been Burnley's banning of individual reporters, and newspapers, from the Press box because of what the club's chairman has regarded as improper trespass on club affairs; Arsenal banned Danny Blanchflower, in his capacity as a sportswriter; the Football League, in wintry discontent in 1968, called upon all League clubs to deny Press facilities to any representative of *The People*, after the newspaper had published a series on the drinking capacity and bedroom manners of one of Stockport County's players. This last instance offended British newspapermen more than any of the others had, and rightly. Men who had for years subdued their irritation, even anger, at individual acts of petty arrogance towards them by directors, managers and players, to say nothing of having underplayed the drabness of many games, suddenly saw their friends publicly reproved by the sport for someone else's business conduct. It really is intolerable that sports reporters should be denied facilities to follow their trade just because they work for an employer who has bought some raffish reading material from a footballer.

Football clubs get the sort of publicity from newspapers which is granted to no other sport; naturally so, since football is public property, nourished and cherished to a degree matched nowhere else. If the League were to follow the principle of banning newspapers every time they gossip unfavourably about the game it would very soon find that the offensive material can outweigh the well-disposed. No newspaper can afford not to write about football, but there are several with the resources and the ruthlessness to dig up and overstress all kinds of little sins scattered about the game should they feel sufficiently provoked. I am thinking of illicit payments to greedy players, irregularities in the sale of tickets for big matches, sweetening of fathers in the bargaining for the signatures of promising boy-players, boardroom politics which squeeze out the directors who ask the awkward questions, rancour in the dressing-rooms, players' late nights and gambling debts. Newspapers do not delve into matters like these any more deeply than is sufficient to handle the stories when they occasionally emerge because sports staffs are in the main much more interested in the game. What is more they accept that a degree of this kind of blemish is inevitable in any commercial enterprise as glamorous and as fiercely contested as is professional football. The League's display of pious horror when a vulgar newspaper occasionally tells all about very little is a grotesque mistake. I suspect the public wonders what the League is frightened of rather than agrees that the newspaper should be censured.

There have, of course, been one or two serious revelations by the Press of scandalous misconduct in football, most notably *The People*'s exposures of instances of conspiracy in result-fixing and of stimulant-drug taking, and more recently the same paper's naming of a leading ticket tout with many embarrassing connections in the game. Stories like these must damage football, but not nearly as much as the improprieties would if allowed to grow unseen. There is no point in venting bitterness on the men who reveal the graft. It is not usually the sports reporters who hold it up for the public to inspect because the unpleasantness the investigation involves would cut off the ready access they need for their bread and butter information. They may supply the news editor with addresses and telephone numbers, but they do not often handle the eavesdropping tape-recorders themselves.

Football clubs, and particularly their managers, are notoriously fickle friends to sportswriters. They regard them mostly as tame publicists, and some managers look for a discretion in reporters' handling of their frankness which they judge story by story. Generally, the stronger the manager the less reticent he is when talking to reporters and the less sensitive to what they write. But with some managers the reporter walks a tightrope between their equivocation and their secretiveness. To be told nothing is less exasperating than to be told, after the story has appeared: 'I *know* I said it, but I didn't expect you to *print* it.'

There are managers who can never be reached by telephone and can only be spoken to in an atmosphere of papal audience after a wait of hours. I remember being told by one manager, not at all well placed in Division Two, that he was not interested in talking to me because 'newspaper features don't seem to do me any good'. How's that for a voice from an entertainment industry?

The language of football reporting has long been an attractive target for pedants, and privately for football writers themselves. The nature of the game encourages emotive words, staccato phrases, comparison with war. The swelling thunder of the crowd, the mixture of the graceful and the frantic on the field, the deep-lying involvement in the game on the part of the spectator, all insist on a florid content in the prose.

Much football writing is done when the reporter is in a state of some excitement, when the din of a huge crowd is making his temples twang. This is not the sweet, contemplative atmosphere in which cricket reporters may place their adverbs with the infinite care of a late cut. The football reporter is frequently frozen to the bone, so that words become petrified in his head like that famous toothpaste tube advertised in a block of ice. Press boxes are not the ivory towers that some critics perceive when they sit down to write their thousand-word letters of sneering comment to our editors. The boxes may often be quite high up in the air, but they induce more lifted pulses than lofty thoughts.

Readers of sports pages can be surprisingly arch. I once wrote a reference to a crowd of Liverpool supporters singing dirges and chanting graffiti, and received a letter from the senior common room of the School of Management at Bath University of Technology, inviting me to arrange 'an evening's chanting of unusual scribblings', as if this was ever such a cutting joke. Aware of the licence I had claimed for the use of the word, I was much less self-critical about it than I was the day I dictated the poor, pawed old line, 'the bubbling cauldron that is Anfield', as if it was new.

But it must be admitted that the student of the language has plenty to clout when he looks at football writing. Our sports pages are weighted with brawny scoring aces, they trip over our breakfasts on the heels of impish little baggy-pants geniuses, they glower with veteran centre-halves who silence elfin forwards like severe schoolmasters, and they drip with the blood of mud-caked battles *almost* reminiscent of the Somme. Every other teenage newcomer to a team's forward line either gives the opposing defence a lesson or gets one from it. Chelsea's forward, Peter Osgood, was Sogood; Manchester United's opponents were lucky not to suffer six of the Best. Red-haired players are fiery, little ones big-hearted, big ones gentle giants. Managers never *say* anything, but snap, declare, deny or challenge. Musically minded reporters tell us frequently that they have just seen a team bewitched, bothered and bewildered or looking like an orchestra without a conductor. Referees, I am bound to agree, usually are either imperious or indecisive.

Well, at least it is a substantial improvement on all that more pompous stuff I remember seeing twenty-five years ago about custodians punching the spheroid from the centre-forward's head. Play may still be end to end now and again, but it no longer ensues, which is an advance. The odd colossus still makes an appearance, striding the midfield, although he is more popular with the lads in the supporters' club bar than with reporters lately. It is some time since I read of any defence making good its motto, Thou Shalt Not Pass, but there seems to be a welter of teams which, though not great sides themselves, it will take a great side to beat.

The trouble with most football prose is that it is deliberately aimed downwards with a flourish, the assumption being that the distraught, swearing fan on the terraces is exactly the same mindless creature when he coughs over his newspaper in the bleak of the morning tea break. It is curious that football reporters very seldom use the same language in talking about the game that they employ when writing about it. No reporter has ever in his life stood with his back to the bar and a pint of bitter in his hand and said in all seriousness that a forward line moved as if Younger than Springtime, or that an inside forward was a little general with dynamite in his boots.

There is a quality of pain in football which strikes a chord of memory in spectators', and reporters', responses, and I think it is this that imposes a continuing thread of sentimentality in the reporting of the game. There is a great deal of affection for youth in it. ('Boys in blue' was frequently used in reference to a very young Manchester City side; 'The Busby Babes', the nickname for the Manchester United team destroyed at Munich, is the classic example.) The language has developed into a distinctive style, part melodrama, part slop. Just as football seen in edited, compressed version on television has become commonly recognized as a distortion for which viewers make allowances, so has newspaper reporting of matches become accepted as an entertainment in its own right. It is deliberately overdrawn because while football matches are sometimes dull sports pages can never afford to be.

This does not, of course, excuse some of the lurching alliteration (careful now, Mr Critic) which has fullbacks bamboozled by the best of Busby's brilliant bunch, or some of the mixing of metaphors, by which youngsters thrown in at the deep end emerge from the water having won their spurs. But I cannot deny that I shall be always grateful to the evening paper reporter who added three of the best-loved clichés together and thus constructed a figure of irresistible appeal. Ray Wilson, the Everton and England fullback, he wrote, was not only one of the first gentlemen of the game but he walked tall in soccer's top drawer. That, we surely must admit, wins the accolade.

8 Football and Foreigners

British arrogance has been reflected vividly, and calamitously, in football. Our islanders' insularity, our lingering conviction of international, and natural, superiority, blinded us until very recent years to the bounding developments in the game in other countries. It is astonishing to recall, now that we have made a typically aggressive recovery so that we half believe we invented the changes, that it needed other Europeans to teach us about floodlights and midweek night matches, about tactical defence in depth, about lightweight athletes' clothing for playing the game in – and about paying footballers the kind of wages which match their commercial worth as entertainers.

Before the last war our domestic competitions absorbed us almost totally. The English, Welsh, Scottish and Northern Irish associations withdrew from FIFA, the world football authority, before the World Cup was instituted in 1930, and we ignored this tournament, as if it were some slightly comic argument being conducted on the fringes of *our* sport, for twenty years.

Games between British teams and other nations' were faintly curious 'friendlies', in which extremely violent incidents could sometimes occur, as when Eddie Hapgood had his nose broken by a deliberate punch from an Italian player in 1934. We were mostly concerned, when we talked about 'international' matches, with the ones between England and Scotland, England

and Wales, England and Ireland. It was always a matter of whether the underprivileged Celts could humble the pride of the country which was unquestionably assumed to be the world's champion at football. All this time the foreigners were refurbishing the game, adding more ordered, physical commitment to it, more collective flair, more general smartness, taking some of the solemnity out of it, removing some of the apparent immutables, like the institution of the purely defensive fullback. It was all happening in Italy and Spain, in Eastern Europe and in South America, and for most Britons jammed tight in their favourite football grounds every Saturday afternoon, and reading every word of the sports pages, it went entirely unnoticed.

We entered the World Cup for the first time in 1950, and I remember as a teenager at the time being none too sure whether this was something to do with the Olympic Games or not. In any case, when I saw we had a match to play against the USA in a town in Brazil whose name I had to mumble to avoid admitting mispronunciation, I regarded the matter as of only passing interest. The Americans beat England 1–0. Amazement was followed by a sense of outrage, as if the country had been betrayed by its government and delivered up to the khaki invader we thought we had sent back to Brooklyn and Texas five years before. I abandoned my pen-pal in Massachusetts as a reprisal.

The fifties relentlessly exposed the lie we had been cherishing as noble truth for so long. We could not play football better than any other country, after all. Far from knowing all there was to be known about the game we found that we had been left years behind by it. We even looked old. Our shorts were longer, thicker, flappier than anyone else's, so that our players looked like Scoutmasters struggling to keep pace with the troop.

We lost dignity in our disorder, blatantly shoving with our hands at nimbler players as they went past. The dull training routines, aimed at deep chests and stamina and doggedness, had done exactly what they were intended to do. Hungary, with a marvellous constellation of players grouped around Puskas and Hidegkuti, crushed us 6–3 on a November afternoon at Wembley in 1953, and in the following year stamped us into the ground with a 7–1 win in Budapest. We have always been aware of our capacity for laughing at ourselves, but the degree of self-derision in which we were now invited to indulge was beyond us. It was left to the spirit of individual clubs to redeem the reputation of the national sport.

Matt Busby, in creating the young Manchester United team of the mid fifties, is due every kind of gratitude from British football: he gave us back lost pride, pleasure and understanding. Incredibly, authority in the form of the Football League still behaved as if competition in international football was no more than an irritating interruption of its programme. The League audaciously told Chelsea, the club champions when the European Cup was begun in 1955, that they were to refuse the invitation to take part. The Scottish League allowed Hibernian, of Edinburgh, to compete and the club surprised Europe by reaching the semi-finals. The following season Busby coldly ignored the Football League's instruction not to enter his championship side in the tournament, and United also reached the semi-finals. They lost on an aggregate score of 5–3 in the two matches to the overall strength and flair of Real Madrid, the greatest club side of the decade, which won the European Cup five times in succession.

Manchester United brought a high flame of hope back to British football. In 1956 they beat Anderlecht, of Belgium, 10–0, which was the sort of thing any decent Briton had always expected of his footballers when confronted with people from the other side of the Channel, and later on they put three goals past Bilbao in Spain and another three in Manchester. Not only was United's football thrillingly attractive but it could be crushingly effective. It took the sourness out of our view of our own game, even if authority still had its stubborn old head in the domestic sand.

The United team was on its way home from Belgrade, having won through to the semi-finals of the European Cup once again, in 1958, when it was destroyed in the air crash at Munich. In the years immediately following, Wolves, Burnley and Tottenham Hotspur represented England, Spurs delighting us in 1961 with a resounding 8–1 defeat of Gornik, of Poland, and going out in the semi-finals to the eventual winners, Benfica, of Portugal.

By the mid sixties British football, having borrowed hungrily from other countries' method and even character, and at last having adapted and shaped the polymath to a creation appropriate to its own tradition and temperament, was recognized as a major international force again. West Ham United won the European Cupwinners' Cup with an incisive grace in 1965, beating Munich 1860 by 2–0 in the final at Wembley; Liverpool lost the final of the same competition by 2–1 to Borussia Dortmund the following year. Then, in 1967, Celtic of Glasgow crowned Britain's post-war performance in international club football with a devastating flow of attacking play to beat Internazionale, of Italy, 2–1 in the final of the European Cup.

I have already commented, in a profile of Sir Alf Ramsey, the England team manager, on England's victory in the World Cup in 1966. But there are social aspects of that competition, whose last rounds were played in England, which deserve mention because of what they say about contemporary British

attitudes to football, and especially to footballing foreigners.
To begin with the competition released in our country a communal exuberance which I think astonished ourselves more
than our visitors. It gave us a chance to spruce up a lot, to
lighten the leaden character of the grounds where the matches
were played, to throw off much of our inhibition of behaviour,
particularly in the provinces, so that we became a gay, almost
reckless people in our own streets, which is commonly only
how we conduct ourselves when we put on our raffia hats in
other countries' holiday resorts. Except in the celebrations that
greeted the end of the Second World War, I have never seen
England look as unashamedly delighted by life as it did during
the World Cup.

This was, of course, the true England of the industrial
provinces, of blood-black brick and scurrying wind and workers'
faces clenched tight against the adversity of short-time working
and the memory of last month's narrow miss on the pools;
our best football is not played in the bland England, that
Camelot of the advertisements in overseas' magazines. The
World Cup was carnival. Here was the apotheosis of the game
which lives like an extra pulse in the people of industrial
England.

The English team was playing all·its matches in London,
so that all the games in Liverpool, Manchester, Sunderland,
Middlesbrough, Sheffield and Birmingham were of immediate
interest only in deciding who might oppose us in the final,
assuming that Ramsey's assurance that we would be in it, and
win it, held good. The crowds at the matches were not always
vast – less than 30,000 to see Portugal beat Hungary in one
of the potentially most attractive ties of the tournament at
Old Trafford, under 14,000 for the North Korea *v* Chile game
at Middlesbrough – but in the main they were well up to the

standards of the higher reaches of domestic football. There were 45,000 people to see West Germany play Spain at Villa Park (Birmingham), 32,000 to see Argentina play Switzerland at Sheffield, and at Goodison Park, Everton's ground, the crowds responded with relish to the prospect of Brazil v Bulgaria (47,000), Hungary v Brazil (51,000) and Portugal v Brazil (58,000).

The spectators were watching unfamiliar players, as well as a handful of the ones whom they knew well enough were among the world's finest. With few ready-made favourites to cheer at the matches they quickly appointed their heroes and their villains, and settled their fondness and their disgust upon them without stint. How handsomely the Liverpool crowd saluted the sinuous power and deadly instinct for destruction of Portugal's Eusebio, and how they embraced Hungary's Albert with their delight at his dagger-like thrusts through the Brazilian defence.

And then there was the delirious affection which the Middlesbrough crowd developed for the tiny North Koreans, with their extraordinary three-part names – Li Chan Myung, Han Bong Zin, Lim Zoong Sun, Oh Yoon Kyung – who were billeted at the local airport. This team of tireless, brave gymnasts, who started in a state of obvious bewilderment at the stern orderliness and practised cunning of European and South American football, learned rapidly from one match to another. When they beat Italy 1–0 to win a place in the quarter finals, the crowd fell upon them in hysterical acclaim. My lasting memory of that match is of a tall British sailor lugging two Koreans off the pitch, one under each arm, like prizes. The Koreans' team manager, Mr Kim Eung Su, when asked afterwards what he wanted to say about his players' quite remarkable performance, replied with touching sincerity, which gained in point by the delay in interpretation, that the Koreans 'thank the peoples of Middlesbrough very much'.

These World Cup matches had all the anger, the soaring tension, the love of triumph and the pathos of defeat that attend the football which British crowds follow week by week. Watching these crowds absorbed as if personally involved in these confrontations of foreign teams it seemed unbelievable that only a few years before the national leadership of our game had turned a cold shoulder to organized international competition. This public response confirmed conclusively that football belongs to the people, that it is the conflict and the setting which possess them in their ownership. In a matter of days a dark, slant-eyed footballer with a name like a nonsense rhyme can be adopted as a personal representative by a Middlesbrough labourer just because he is expressing hope and liberation through the one art the labourer fully comprehends. It often sounds unduly pompous and pious when men talk ceremonially about football's role as a bridge across national frontiers. But that is because the occasions of such statements are usually pompous, and so turn a decent truth into a banality. East and West were undoubtedly linked at Middlesbrough.

In the final at Wembley on July 30, 1966, England and West Germany met in circumstances of barely tolerable emotional tension. I have earlier described the closing minutes of this match. But I want to refer to something in its atmosphere which disconcerted me because of its inappropriateness to the game as a whole: the measure of chauvinism which was divorced entirely from what took place, in terms of football, on the field.

I watched this game not from the Press box but from a seat in the stands, and I was struck well before the game began by the unusual nature of some of the crowd around me. They were not football followers. They kept asking each other about the identity of the English players. Wasn't one of the Manchester boys supposed to be pretty good? That very tall chap had a brother in the side, hadn't he? They were there in their rugby club blazers, and with their Home Counties accents and obsolete prejudices, to see the successors of the Battle of Britain pilots whack the Hun again. Some of them wept a bit at the end, and they sang *Land of Hope and Glory* with a solemn fervour I have known elsewhere only at Conservative party rallies. I suspect that if they had found themselves sitting among a crowd of real, live football fans from Liverpool they might have been amazed by the degree of treacherous support available to Jerry. Some football fans prefer even German footballers to plump-living countrymen exercising the privilege of money to bag a place at an event thousands more would have given their right arms to see – and understand. I much prefer *Abide With Me* at Wembley. Its connection with chapel and pub identifies it with the England which nurtures its football.

This is not a complaint against national commitment in sport: that, on the part of Ramsey and his team, greatly helped to win us the championship. But I did resent something discordant in the tone of that climactic afternoon. I wish the terraces of Anfield, Old Trafford, Roker Park and Molyneux had been so heavily represented at Wembley as to overwhelm those decently educated voices of ignorance. I gulped and shouted like everyone else, and congratulated myself on being English with all the acclamation at my command. But it has always nagged at my fond recollection of that day that a lot of my companions might as well have been at Wimbledon.

But at least the art had been properly scrutinized up at Liverpool and Middlesbrough. And had I not heard a tiny English boy ask the trainer of Brazil's team in their Cheshire hotel whether Pele was coming home for his tea? People of that child's generation will never go to Wembley with yester-day's old war wounds in their hearts.

The 1966 World Cup attracted a lot of North American atten-tion. I remember an American journalist, in a state of grace about the Wembley matches, assuring me that within a few years the game would sweep his country. He was talking about 'goalminders' and 'umpires' but he had certainly done his homework about overlapping defenders and other of the main attacking features of the tournament. Since then a great deal of money has been put into promoting the game in the US, but at the time of writing it seems to be poised motionless in its trajectory. Will it carry on upwards, or will it slide back to earth again?

The beginnings of competitive football in the US have been bedevilled by the commercial opportunism which characterizes the nation and which also troubles its other sports, notably boxing. Football began in the country with two rival leagues, which was not healthy for such a young sport. The new Ameri-can clubs recruited expensively from Europe and South Ameri-ca, most of the players they acquired being of an age when they were heading for retirement or coaching jobs. The new financial rewards open to leading British players in their own country made sure that there would be no heightened version of the emigration to Italy that occurred in the previous decade.

But it seems so far that American soccer has not yet progressed beyond the stage of curiosity. In the summer of 1967 sizeable crowds were commanded by a kind of exhibition league, in which foreign clubs, including Wolverhampton Wanderers, Stoke City, ADO of Holland and Bangu of Brazil assumed the temporary titles of American clubs and turned out full strength sides. The names under which they played reflect brightly enough the vivacious style America expects of its soccer: Dallas Tornadoes, Chicago Mustangs, New York Skyliners. Lots of groups of pretty girls whooped up enthusiasm with prancing rallying cries, wearing spangly ice-skating skirts. The atmosphere of the matches was shriller and more light-hearted than is produced by the crowds in the countries of longstanding football tradition.

I must admit immediately that I am commenting not from first-hand experience of American soccer. I have, however, discussed it with a number of men who have played in it and watched it, and it does seem that the circus or showbiz element attached to the introduction of the game, in an effort to make it quickly appealing to people who know nothing about it, has not really helped.

I think it is significant that football, in every country where it commands national attention, is never a particularly pretty, decorative affair. In Britain various clubs have experimented with little dancing shows as appetizers for football crowds: groups of girls doing hip-swinging marching routines to pop music; live pop groups belting out the Top Ten into amplifiers on stages placed on the touchline. They have seldom attracted much commendation. They are an attempt to update, for the pleasure of the younger fans, the tradition of live entertainment which used to be maintained by solemn brass bands and military drummers. Even in Brazil, where the temperament is as sympathetic to a touch of girly show as can possibly be expected, this kind of crowd sweetener has not proved valuable. The point about football is football. It can have its own comicality, its own glamour and appeal to the senses; but if it cannot make its own living no amount of decoration will turn it into a magnet.

In the US, of course, films of the World Cup matches and

then games played between visiting teams of high quality from other countries have been followed by less skilful, slower contests between domestic teams, stiffened by ageing players bought from outside. The comparison, even to spectators who are not familiar with the sport, is obviously damaging to the domestic leagues. I know enough of the American capacity for conjuring instant success in brand new fields not to dismiss the possibility of rapid development of soccer in the US. But there are heavy reservations against such a proposition. The game, at its best, is the most exciting sport the world has: but there is no point in denying that it can be drab lower down the scale.

Local commitment can sustain teams of poor quality, but mostly because of memory of better days, the habit of attendance and because of a context in which such second- and third-grade teams may occasionally be allowed to lift their performance to challenge much better ones – as in national cup competitions. Without these provisions drab teams are seen always as drab teams. In England's Third and Fourth Divisions some clubs play regularly in front of between 3,000 and 6,000 people. The American clubs will need much bigger crowds than that to satisfy the promoters that they have a commercial property. I wonder whether the promoters have the patience to wait for the general standard of the game to improve sufficiently to guarantee potential spectators something reasonably describable as spectacular.

Americans have told me that soccer has great appeal among schools because it is such a suitable game for boys of varying size and physical strength; because the American football of the padded uniforms and crash helmets has become so much like trench warfare that it is increasingly unacceptable to teachers and parents. They argue, too, that soccer's continuous movement makes it more appealing than baseball. Plainly, if

H

the game that the rest of the world calls football were to become widely played in American schools its development as an adult sport would be assured. But again the question poses itself: will the promoters wait for that?

The US, in beating England in the 1950 World Cup, suggested a dramatic boosting of the game in their country on the way. It did not materialize. I do not think that dramatic take-off is possible, even in a country where wealth and energy can exploit new enthusiasms so readily. If the US becomes enthralled by soccer it will be when every other back street and stretch of urban waste ground has its teams of kids playing their makeshift matches, the players claiming the temporary identity of the world's stars in the sport.

Environments like that produce those stars. Football is an inner compulsion. It cannot be settled on a people like instant coffee. The world must wish the game well in the US; but the only way it can properly grow is to start in the cradle.

9 The Future

In this last chapter I want to consider some of the effects of the particular situations I have been describing, and suggest a few of the trends which are likely to be significant in British football in the coming years. If we look at what has happened in the professional game since the early fifties we can see clearly enough that dramatic developments are possible in a very short time. In this respect football has been no different from many other influences on daily life, whether road transport, license in the theatre or adolescents' wages.

The whole appearance and manner of professional football have been transformed, not to everybody's liking. The youthfulness of a team, as a positive policy rather than as an enforced result of a high incidence of injury, is now a commonplace; even Third and Fourth Division clubs adopt it. The game is played at sprinter's pace; it is more explosive than it was; players are cunning veterans by their mid-twenties; referees are frequently treated with undisguised contempt; managers grow more tense and anxious by the month; the conflict between the younger and older generations, which is one of the major contemporary tensions in society generally, is given emphatic expression in football. Even boards of directors are beginning to get younger.

In an attempt to clarify the problems I shall discuss them in compartments.

1 'New Deal' — and aftermath

One of the main props of the Football League's case when it
opposed the 'New Deal' for players was that to abolish the
maximum wage and allow men freer movement from one club
to another would be to threaten the very existence of the smaller
clubs, simply because they would be priced out of business. The
suggestion was that before long the only towns with fulltime
professional football would be those which could command huge
audiences from surrounding areas of heavy population. Have
these fears been proved justified, and if not is it likely that they
will be soon? Secondly, would it be a bad thing if they were?

The two most important points about professional football are
surely that a large number of men should play it and a large
number of people watch it. Anything which reduces either
number must be bad for the game. But that having been agreed
there are certain qualifications which must be made. To begin
with the players insisted on, and secured, high wages and
freedom to negotiate contracts with their employers because
the restraint imposed on them had become intolerable to a
society with any pretension to a belief in justice. Secondly,
there is no law either of statute or nature which says that people
have got to go on watching their town football club even when
it bores them. Thirdly, good players enjoy their football most
when they play with good teams, and there is no defensible
case for placing obstacles to frustrate the joining of the two.
Fourthly, the mobilization of previously static, provincial
communities is one of the characteristic aspects of our national
life in this half of the century, and football will do better to
adapt to it instead of regretting it.

It is not at all to the credit of the member clubs of the Football

League, or to the management of the League, that spectators were for years treated with scant concern. The wages clubs paid until 1961 made little inroad on the takings at the turnstiles in all those boom years immediately before and after the war, when people habitually turned out in tens of thousands to watch local football in conditions of considerable squalor. Some clubs may like to consider how much the condition of lavatories, stands and terraces contributed to the alienation of supporters once the television set and the car admitted the working-classes over the threshold of comfortable diversion. So where did the money go, since much of it was not spent on either of the two prime components of the game, players and spectators? In too many cases it seems that it went nowhere at all, but simply lay about, as if under the mattress, until the rising cost of living and unimaginative management ate it up.

There are small clubs lately which, by the bold and business-like attack of young directors and astute managers, have rapidly escaped from apparent decomposition into energy and actual profit. They have done it by recognizing the needs of the decade and meeting them. The consistently successful clubs command massive attendances by the spectacle they can offer in terms of excitement on the field. Where the football is less glamorous, and cash short, the sensible club offers spectators comfort above the average; it actively seeks to engage their interest in the running of things; it trades in players with extra care; it streamlines its playing and scouting staffs to concentrate maximum effort on the immediate object, which may be to win promotion or avoid relegation.

It is the club which is prepared to find its own solution to its own particular problems, instead of stumbling along with attitudes which time has overtaken, which excites local interest. It is intensely irritating that clubs which have been vigorous enough, and clear-sighted enough, to innovate instead of crumble – Coventry City and Stockport County, for example, both resuscitated brashly; Walsall and Portsmouth, both lifted by a specialist form of work-study applied to team building – have all been accused by grey-heads in the game of 'gimmickry'. There are two main objects in professional football: to put the ball into the other team's net and to make people watch you do it. Any club which rediscovers a lost capacity for both deserves every encouragement.

It seems to me irrelevant to complain that small clubs cannot afford to match big clubs' wages. It is much more important to football that its excitement and skill at the top should be assured than that clubs with low resources and low skills should be protected by restrictions imposed on the big ones. The number of youths and men who play organized football, paid and unpaid, up and down the country increases all the time; the number of people who want to watch the defeats of Rochdale, Halifax, Bradford, Chester, Reading, diminishes steadily. The two facts are not unrelated. Interest in football has not declined; interest in paying money to watch an indifferent quality of it undoubtedly has.

What, then, is to happen to these struggling clubs? Cliff Lloyd, the secretary of the Professional Footballers' Association, suggested to me that there may soon be far more part-time footballers than there are now, and the prediction seems a fair one.

I referred in another chapter to clubs like Stafford Rangers who, in the late forties and in modest competitions, could command the sort of crowds Fourth Division clubs often get nowadays. It is not unreal to visualize Third and Fourth Division clubs operating very much like smarter versions of these semi-professionals. There is little chance that attendances in the lower League divisions are going to rise substantially above their present level – on average around 4,000 to 7,000. Costs of running entirely professional football will get higher, not lower. The ambitious clubs, looking for promotion and for good wins in the FA and League Cups, will stay fully professional, and I see no reason for objecting to a situation in which fulltime footballers play part-timers regularly. It is no more a mis-match than putting the non-League clubs in with a chance of beating a leading League club in the FA Cup. There are, already, a number of part-time professionals playing in the lower reaches of the League. My belief is that, in the interest of survival, many of the clubs will adopt the policy as central.

This would, I think, dispel a lot of the confusion of intention among these clubs. It is pointless to argue that it would reduce some of the competitiveness in the divisions; Chester and Exeter and Mansfield are not exactly breathing down Arsenal's neck. Such a recomposition of the clubs might also take some of their devotion to League status off its pedestal and facilitate a readier movement into the League of clubs who already have the adequate resources of income and playing skill. New faces can sometimes revitalize old institutions.

This process will be resisted by the League. Its members guard the ramparts jealously. But circumstances, I believe, will impose it, just as they have imposed a distinct recklessness among clubs in their anxiety to sign up promising boy-players. Sir Stanley Matthews, in trying to revive the sagging condition of Port Vale, embarked boldly on a policy of recruiting schoolboys, so that he might build a brand-new team. Port Vale appeared merely to have circumvented the rules as richer clubs do, but with less stealth.

Semi-professional League clubs, with more realistic ambitions and less need to put up a false front of glamour and opportunity, would be more relaxed and more selective in this kind of recruitment – less concerned with trying to outflank the richer clubs, and with more time to make sure that the boys they acquire are really equipped for professional football. I am sure a lot of parents would prefer to see their sons beginning in this modest way, rather than pitched into the high drama of a leading club and then to suffer the bitter disappointment of failure before they are out of their teens.

At the moment the Third and Fourth Divisions are paying the bigger clubs more in transfer fees than they are making from selling players. But the significant point is that the few young players who are transferred *up* the League fetch individually far bigger sums than the more numerous older ones moving down it. If the small clubs could develop a positive, pragmatic role as finders and sellers of talent their condition would be healthier. The clubs generally resist this idea, stubbornly insisting that they should recruit solely for long-term playing success, rather than do the richer clubs' nursery work for them. But this attitude makes it harder for them to acquire promising young players, because few boys want to be tied to a little club if there is a chance of joining a glamorous one. The small clubs need to concern themselves more with profit and less with status.

How far may this process go? Will the smaller clubs in the Second and First Divisions also have to deny themselves major ambitions? It has to be agreed that clubs such as Burnley, Sheffield United, Huddersfield, Preston, Derby, will always have to concentrate on astute, meagre buying and on turning out home-trained players rather than on heavy dealing in the transfer market; and, again, they may always need to raise money by the tactical selling of players of high ability. But this does not necessarily mean that they may never challenge the biggest clubs for leading honours. Burnley have done it stylishly, even if they have lately slumped. Their problems of comparatively small crowds and resources impose an extra responsibility for tight management; but this can be relished by the right men. It is going to be extremely interesting to watch what happens at Rotherham, where Tommy Docherty, the former Chelsea manager, recently took charge under a board of directors which has given him both rein and an impressive sense of deep, personal involvement. Both Rotherham and Burnley have unpretentious grounds but the very best training facilities. Docherty, at the moment of writing faced with the likely prospect of relegation to Division Three, talks about the equally likely prospect of regular all-ticket sellouts if only he can get the club into Division One in a season or two.*

Many players want to play for Docherty and for other managers of his generation and his urgent commitment to the game. It is not unreasonable to expect that there are going to be enough of such men to manage, or assist in managing, most of the clubs in the top two divisions while they are still visibly young. It is likely that playing careers are going to get shorter; that top players, beginning in their mid-teens and faced every week by the punishing pace of modern football, will commonly retire at 30, rather than gently fade out through the lower divisions around 35, as they used to. It seems equally reasonable that First and Second Division clubs should want to engage some of these highly knowledgeable players as assistant managers at this early age, deliberately pre-training them for special attention to young players because of their closeness to the game and the respect youngsters have for them. There are already signs that this is a likely development in the very near future. Far more clubs than used to care about players' futures now encourage them to take coaching courses seriously. At least

* Rotherham *were* relegated.

one leading First Division club made it plain a while ago that a senior player was in line as its future manager well before he had stopped playing.

This, I believe, is one of the direct results of the players' 'New Deal'. The game has become more important to the players. Because they need to worry less about what will happen to them when they can no longer play they immerse themselves more completely in their football. They are more captive to the game than previous generations.

There was a general expectation a little while ago of what was called a Super League, in which all the leading European clubs would play, breaking away from the domestic leagues in their own countries. It has not materialized, and is not likely to. Cost and the difficulties of travelling, and also the differences in lengths of the seasons in different countries, make the proposition unattractive. In any case, the European Cup, the Cupwinners' Cup and the Inter-Cities Fairs' Cup already seem to provide adequate international football at club level to satisfy the fans. But a more likely suggestion is that a domestic Premier League may hive off from the English Football League to confine top-quality football to perhaps a dozen of the country's major areas of population. This is a perfectly rational idea, and one which is known to find favour among a number of men in influential positions in football.

The argument is that the economics of the game are already imposing just such a 'premier' league *inside* Division One. It is suggested, not without point, that in the next few years the First Division will be seen to be consistently a matter of dispute between those areas whose population alone allows them to sustain the biggest crowds and therefore retain the most gifted players: two clubs each for London and probably Manchester and Liverpool; one each for, say, the central industrial Midlands, the North East, South Yorkshire, West Lancashire, the West Midlands, and perhaps the South coast.

The trouble with this line of thinking is that there would have to be promotion into, and relegation out of, this premier division, otherwise the League would never permit it. For the clubs to break away from the League in order to set it up would require more self-confidence, and more disenchantment with the present opposition, than the richer clubs have. The League's member clubs are never going to agree to any change in organization which would remove the chance of top football an inch further from the Second Division clubs than it is now.

There is surely much to be said for retaining the First and Second Divisions as now constituted. Flair and resolution can often bring considerable success to clubs which have to watch their budgets. Contest is the essence of professional football; and while it is not realistic to talk of sustaining the game indefinitely where the crowds are of 3,000 and 4,000 spectators it is good business sense to keep the rich clubs looking over their shoulders at the healthy, aggressive ones on the way up. Clubs like Burnley, Wolverhampton Wanderers and Sheffield United will repeatedly bring back the lapsed thousands to their grounds, and hold them, whenever they look like winning something. Demoted to a secondary competition in an arrogant, planner's reorganization they would immediately find bigger empty spaces where the fans ought to be, and those spaces might never again be filled.

2 Violent play — and refereeing

Different people have different words for the increasing violence on professional football pitches. A lot of journalists use 'vicious' frequently; managers and players more often say 'petulant'. It is perhaps an instructive comparison. The spectator sees a player swing his right boot at the retreating figure of an opponent, or strike out with a fist when the ball is yards away from him. What the spectator sees is a delayed assault when the referee's back is turned. Players, viewing the game from inside, think they recognize the eruptive reaction of a frustrated man, and perhaps a provoked one. But whatever this violence is called it has too often disfigured the game in recent seasons. What may be done about it?

I have referred in earlier chapters to some of the influences which create anger on the field, and I repeat here that as long as football is something people care deeply about there will always be tension and ill-temper in it. The fierce, reckless tackle by which a tough defender clears a forward out of the path to goal in a desperate disregard of injury has been a feature of football as long as I can remember. The best forwards learn to avoid such tackles as often as to suffer them: that is what makes them top players. The best defenders learn to make them rarely, when the situation leaves them with the choice between conceding personal defeat and making a last-ditch effort to win the fight. These are not the incidents we need to worry about. What gives concern is the deliberate assault that occurs, common lately, when the victim does not have the ball.

For example? In a First Division match in 1968 I watched two defenders sandwich a winger, who had been giving them a deal of trouble, and force him heavily over the by-line. Well, that was a bit of minor rough stuff, hardly unprecedented. But, a moment later when the ball had been cleared well up-field, one of the defenders, as if by afterthought, stamped his right foot hard on the winger's legs as he lay on the ground. A colleague described to me, appalled, after another First Division match, a scene in which a forward, previously fouled by an opponent, ran at the man, jumped high and crashed both feet into his body. Petulant or vicious?

It cannot be stressed enough that the high rewards now available in football – not just in terms of players' pay but in the glamour that goes with winning places in international club tournaments – have added greatly to the tautness of the conflict inherent in the game. But if the accompanying assault and battery cannot be dismissed from it this heightened competitiveness will eventually turn the sport sour.

It is difficult, perhaps impossible, to plot the point at which a game turns nasty. I am writing this section the day after watching a marvellously exciting match between Liverpool and Tottenham Hotspur, an FA Cup fifth round replay in which Liverpool scored the vital goal of the night's three with a penalty which the referee ordered to be taken twice under somewhat arguable circumstances. Spurs' goalkeeper saved the first penalty. It is hard to imagine a situation more likely to produce a flare of bitter aggression on a football field, if winning is the most important influence on players' conduct. But this match was never unpleasant. What fouls were committed arose directly out of the flow of the game. There were no private feuds, no punching on the referee's blind side. Yet on the previous Saturday a First Division club's goalkeeper was sent off the field after striking a Second Division forward in a Cup match, when the senior side was clearly well in command.

Some of the worst incidents of violence on the field have little to do with who is winning. It is inescapable that some clubs are much more ready to fight with their fists and kick opponents gratuitously than others, not for any irritation that develops out of the particular game but because it is borne in their nature. Teams evolve a group character, and it reflects the character of their management. The control of violence on the field surely begins in the dressing-rooms and in the managers' offices, and cannot be the sole responsibility of referees.

It has been suggested that when football's disciplinary committees consider cases in which referees have been shoved about or sworn at, or when players have been sent off for repeated, ugly fouls, judgement should be delivered on the managers of the offending players, and not just on the players themselves. There are even one or two managers who have been prepared to support this view, although most, naturally, can be expected to reject the idea as intolerable. Clearly to punish a manager, either by fine or by brief suspension from the game, for isolated acts of temper by players is out of the question. But is it too much to accept that clubs which are regularly in trouble of this kind ought to be forced to curb their players' excesses? Several times in the 1967-8 season club managers and chairmen have grumbled that players dismissed by referees and punished by authority have been badly treated. The most combative of the fans certainly are delighted by this championing of their favourites, and it is hardly calculated to invite the players to question their own behaviour.

There have been instances of club directors admitting privately that they have been ashamed of the behaviour of some of their own players, while their managers are talking bitterly of other teams' provocation and of demanding personal hearings for their men threatened with suspension. The fact is that directors and managers know they have an influence on how their teams behave on the field. Some managers and coaches confess in private, and without much show of concern, that they have deliberately built up their team's attitude to one of extra belligerence when they have prepared to meet certain other teams.

It is an old ploy, known to generations, to clout an opposing player of gift but insufficient courage hard and early in a game, so as to neutralize him for the rest of it. But this is not the sort of thing we are discussing. Players report hearing opponents instructing each other to 'get' So-and-so, and they mean to have him off the field if possible. It ought to be possible to contest a game hard, even bitterly, without treating it like street-gang warfare. Managements decide the nature of their teams. If some of them persist in encouraging viciousness (or petulance), even if only by their silence, they should surely be discouraged from it by penalty. I venture to suggest that this innovation will eventually be imposed upon football, even though it will be fought hard by the clubs.

Professional footballers are so ready nowadays to treat some referees contemptuously that it quite often appears as if the official is about to be ordered off the field. Sir Stanley Rous, the president of FIFA and once a famous referee, is right when he says it is a matter of urgency that the referee's word should be restored to a position of command. The problem is, as I stated in the chapter on referees, that the quality of refereeing is so variable. The pace and fierceness of the game have overtaken many referees: so many of them, in fact, that it is increasingly apparent that they have overtaken the very institution of the part-time official. The good, fair-minded man of public spiritedness that this luminary is supposed to be simply is not relevant to the game he has to control. He arrives in top-class football in his 30s, having won experience in the public park and the county leagues, having never been involved in the kind of contest he now has to judge.

Professional footballers are uniformly arrogant about their business. Why not? Thousands cheer and boo them, idolize and hate them, and they are deeply conscious, in their triumph and exhaustion, that they alone know exactly how it was that they scored a spectacular goal in circumstances of extreme physical danger, or prevented someone else from doing so. They are specialist athletes who need courage and flair, and they are rebuked, even humiliated now and again, by clerks and other middle-aged 'no-marks' (to borrow a player's unkind epithet), in the face of which they are expected to stay placid and keep their mouths shut. There are referees who recognize the central absurdity of this situation, remain deaf to players' swearing hot-tempered except when it threatens a general disorder, and impose obedience on the field by their own strength of character. There are others who plainly excite anger and confusion by their weakness of will and inappropriate fussing over trivial detail.

The call for fulltime referees has been rejected so far on the grounds that they would cost too much, that there are not enough men willing to take on such a job, that there is no guarantee that a professional referee would be any better than a part-timer. Even referees will advance that last objection. Let us look at the three arguments separately.

The salary for a fulltime referee would have to be commensurate with a fulltime player's, and also that of a leading player's. That means the referee would be paid somewhere between £3,000 and £5,000 a year, the sum probably decided by the number of games he controlled. He ought to get extra money for officiating at the major occasions, such as the FA Cup final and international matches, since he would be selected for such games, as he is now, on merit, as players are.

Before we consider where the money would come from, let's

look at what money is available in football. The leading clubs often bank £12,000 or £15,000 after a home match. Total clubs' takings from matches in the League's top two divisions are around £5,000,000 a season. Even discounting what money may, in future years, be available to professional football administration either from the football pools or from possible central government funds, there is a sizeable sum for use.

Now how many professional referees would we need? It is not realistic to say that all professional football should be handled on the field by a fulltime referee; but it is increasingly obvious that the standard of handling top-class football has got to be raised. If it were agreed that the First and Second Divisions should have professional referees we would need twenty-two a week in England. If we increase this number to a minimum of twenty-five, to allow for sickness and pulled muscles, and if we pay each of them a maximum of £5,000 a year the annual sum required is £125,000. Put this in the perspective of modern football, and it is the transfer fee of a single player of highest quality. Why should such a sum produce a recoil of amazement from the administrators of the game?

Where would these men come from? It would clearly be ridiculous suddenly to appoint twenty-five professional referees from the ranks of the present part-timers, even if there were enough of them ready to take the posts. Some of them have decent jobs of their own, and being already in their late 30s or early 40s would be unlikely to move into employment which would last only a few years. But several of the younger referees now in the League would undoubtedly jump at the job, and they would also be adequate for it.

It has been argued that retired players do not necessarily

make good referees, and that those who might be good enough technically would find it too difficult to make the transition from team-mate to impartial judge. But we are not dealing with large numbers. Is it unreasonable to suggest that there are half a dozen players now nearing retiring age who have the natural intelligence and the integrity to do a referee's job well? Their understanding of the game is surely supremely valuable.

So perhaps we have a dozen men of the suitable knowledge and character readily available, assuming of course that the retired players would undergo some concentrated training in refereeing, and be given at least a season's experience at a lower level. It is not suggested that the twenty-five professional referees should be appointed *en bloc* in July to take over when the next season begins in August. The remainder of the appointments would be made from young men at present refereeing in lower classes of football who would be willing to concentrate solely on the game as long as a career was assured. It is reasonable to suppose that if applicants for these jobs were asked for there would be a heavy response. Some very close sifting ought to produce the right men. The task then would be to train them hard and specifically for top-class football.*

If we envisage refereeing as a job there is no reason why it should not give a man highly paid work for about fifteen years, the average length of a player's career. He would be under contract to the League, or perhaps to the FA, who would pay him directly, regardless of where Authority got the money from – whether from special levies on clubs or from central funds.

* The Chester Report on football, prepared for the Government in 1968, was against full-time referees but advocated a small cadre of leading part-timers who would get retainers of £1,000 a year and would handle the major matches.

Would the professional be necessarily better than the part-timer? Surely he would. He would be expected to be physically fit for the job; he would be technically trained for it, constantly informed of developments in the playing of the game. Merely the uninterrupted association with the game ought logically to add much to his understanding of it. He could afford to be unquestionable on the field because the players would recognize his professional status. He would be accepted by the players as part of the game and not resented as an outsider.

It might take two or three seasons to introduce the professional referee once the intention had been announced and applications received. There might well be deep disappointment, and a sense of hurt, among current referees of long experience who would find themselves rejected from top-class football. Admittedly this interim period might test to the full the truth of that position claimed for the part-timer of the honest public servant looking for scant reward. But the institution of the professional referee would at last recognize the fact that many of our leading referees have always been frustrated fulltimers, caring little about their regular jobs, but inadequately trained for football and meanly paid. Is it not time refereeing caught up with the game?

So I have reached, at the end, a note of anxious complaint. That is not inappropriate in a book by a football fan. I said at the beginning that the game compelled scrutiny and not just blind acceptance.

I have tried to salute football while remaining as watchful for its blemishes as affection allows. I am not sure whether I am congratulating myself or the sport the more when I say that football excites me as much now as it used to in the days when I was quite convinced I would one day play on Wolverhampton

Wanderers' right wing. Sprinting wingers, with unfailing aim for the far, top corner of the net, were as glamorous as Flash Gordon when I was 12 years old.

Even now, whenever I arrive at any football ground, or merely pass close to one when it is silent, I experience a unique alerting of the senses. The moment evokes my past in an instantaneous emotional rapport which is more certain, more secret, than memory.

Index

Index